Who
Says
I'm an
Addict?

Who Says I'm an Addict?

A book for anyone who is partial to
food, sex, booze or **drugs**

David Smallwood
Former Head of the Addiction Treatment Programme at
the Priory Hospital North London

With Gary Thompson

HAY HOUSE

Carlsbad, California • New York City • London • Sydney
Johannesburg • Vancouver • Hong Kong • New Delhi

First published and distributed in the United Kingdom by:
Hay House UK Ltd, Astley House, 33 Notting Hill Gate, London W11 3JQ
Tel: +44 (0)20 3675 2450; Fax: +44 (0)20 3675 2451
www.hayhouse.co.uk

Published and distributed in the United States of America by:
Hay House Inc., PO Box 5100, Carlsbad, CA 92018-5100
Tel: (1) 760 431 7695 or (800) 654 5126
Fax: (1) 760 431 6948 or (800) 650 5115
www.hayhouse.com

Published and distributed in Australia by:
Hay House Australia Ltd, 18/36 Ralph St, Alexandria NSW 2015
Tel: (61) 2 9669 4299; Fax: (61) 2 9669 4144
www.hayhouse.com.au

Published and distributed in the Republic of South Africa by:
Hay House SA (Pty) Ltd, PO Box 990, Witkoppen 2068
Tel/Fax: (27) 11 467 8904
www.hayhouse.co.za

Published and distributed in India by:
Hay House Publishers India, Muskaan Complex, Plot No.3, B-2,
Vasant Kunj, New Delhi 110 070
Tel: (91) 11 4176 1620; Fax: (91) 11 4176 1630
www.hayhouse.co.in

Distributed in Canada by:
Raincoast Books, 2440 Viking Way, Richmond, B.C. V6V 1N2
Tel: (1) 604 448 7100; Fax: (1) 604 270 7161; www.raincoast.com

Text © David Smallwood and Gary Thompson, 2014

The moral rights of the author have been asserted.

A catalogue record for this book is available from the British Library.

ISBN: 978-1-78180-409-4

Printed and bound in Great Britain by TJ International Ltd, Padstow, Cornwall

Contents

Foreword

Dr Neil Brener, MBBS, MRCPsych

The world of addiction treatment is changing. The concept of what addiction is, and how it affects the lives of individuals and their families, has become more prominent, and this has allowed treatment programmes to develop.

Up until recently, there has been a misperception in the medical profession that detoxification from a drug is tantamount to a treatment programme. Outcome results have therefore been poor, and this has led to a debate around total abstinence versus controlled use and harm reduction.

Due to changes in our understanding of addiction via a better understanding of the neuropathology (how the brain chemistry works), we are starting to re-evaluate this. If we start from the premise that addiction is much wider than just drug and alcohol problems, and includes areas such as gambling, codependency, eating disorders and some sexual behaviour, we start to see that addiction includes both chemical *and* behavioural addiction.

We then have to start thinking about where this all comes from. Not all of it can be explained by neurochemistry – some of it comes from an understanding of a person's emotional world. Ideas around this are also changing.

For the understanding of the treatment of addiction, we need to constantly re-evaluate what we do. Over the years, I have been an exponent of trying out different treatment modalities to aid the addict's recovery. This has led to the introduction of different types of treatment, including equine therapy and trauma work.

From working in the addiction field for a number of years now, I have always been struck by the idea that addiction is a progressive, fatal illness. It is not only destructive to the individual, but it can also have devastating effects on family, children, the workplace and society at large. If we accept this, the goal that we must always be working towards with our patients is total abstinence in all of the multifaceted ways that addiction can present.

The addictive process is 'sneaky', and when you feel you have it under control, it can emerge in other forms, such as over-exercising, workaholism, etc.

It is essential that the whole patient is treated, rather than just their drug or alcohol issues. While this is all happening, there has to be some help and support for families if the addict is going to make a sustained recovery. The more a family understands about the problems, and how they can contribute to the recovery, the more likely it is to happen and be sustained.

I feel we're on the cusp of the medical profession and politicians seeing addiction differently. Hopefully this will be a catalyst for more treatment to become available to members of the public and their families.

All too often, addiction treatment has been seen as a method for reducing crime, and while this is, of course, important, it doesn't take into account the devastating effect of addiction on individuals' lives. When the addiction pebble is dropped in the river, the subsequent ripples affect us all in different ways.

I got into working in addiction by mistake. It has always been seen as one of the Cinderella subjects of psychiatry, but it is amazing when you see a patient turn their life around from their active addiction into an abstinence/recovery. The effect it has on them and everybody around them is transforming and a joy to behold.

I believe that books like *Who Says I'm An Addict* will help people to understand what addiction is, enable them to recognize it in all its forms, and allow people into therapy to make this transformation. I have worked with David Smallwood for many years, and have found his approach to be a constant revelation into our understanding of the devastating effects that addiction has on individuals, families and society.

I hope that his book will be a stepping stone for many people to get further help and support in their recovery.

Dr Neil Brener is a consultant psychiatrist with over 25 years' experience of working with adult patients in the UK's National Health Service, and in the private sector.

Part One

. . . .

Understanding
Addiction

Chapter 1

Why Do I Always Want More?

Most alcoholics will regularly go out with the absolute intention and firm belief that they'll only drink two or three beers. Yet *ten* drinks later they're staggering home, despite the fact that they never planned to get smashed.

I don't think I ever *meant* to get wasted, apart from on two occasions. One was the day I got married and the other was the day my daughter was born (strangely, on neither occasion did I really get that drunk). But there were plenty of times when I'd go to the pub, bump into somebody I knew, and use that as an excuse to go off on a huge drinking binge.

A lot of heavy drinkers will relate to this, if they're honest. The night begins so well, and you fully intend to take it easy. But inevitably, almost before you notice it, one drink has become four and four soon becomes a blur. That quick drink after work unexpectedly turns into a late-night session.

I know people who are constantly late for family gatherings – and also regularly miss important business meetings – because they never seem able to leave the pub on time. They curse themselves for it afterwards, yet it keeps on happening. That first drink might be great, and the second and third ones are wonderful, but by the end of the night they've had *way* too many. Occasionally, they might manage to stay on the straight and narrow, but sooner or later they slip back into their old ways.

Addiction Has No 'off' Button

Interestingly, this urge to consume *more* isn't confined to alcoholics. It affects everybody from time to time, regardless of age or background. For example, how often have you sat on the sofa to relax with a guilty treat – a bar of chocolate, say, or one of your favourite cookies? You fully intend to enjoy it, but at the same time you're determined not to make a pig of yourself. You're adamant that you'll just have a small portion: surely that won't do any harm? The first bite is delicious:

Mmm... it's so tasty. Maybe another bite won't hurt? Oh, go on then, just one more.

Before you know it, you've polished off the whole lot and you're left wondering how your good intentions vanished like a wisp of smoke. Does this sound familiar? Well, we've probably all experienced similar moments.

For most people this sort of behaviour is probably the exception rather than the rule, and it doesn't adversely affect the quality of their everyday life. But for addicts it's very different, because it becomes a compulsion that they simply can't control. Whenever I picked up a drink, I couldn't predict the outcome of events – apart from the fact that more often than not, things would end in chaos. I didn't mean to get drunk; it just happened.

Similarly, someone who's addicted to sex probably doesn't wake up with the intention of sleeping around, but during the course of the day they find themselves in a situation where they feel unable to resist the urge. If, in the morning, you ask them: 'Are you planning to watch pornography today, or maybe have a one night stand this evening?' they'll say 'No' – and they fully believe they're telling the truth.

These weird behaviours exist in lots of different areas of our lives. These days, my favourite addictive substance is sugar. I can go to a restaurant intending to order a balanced meal, because I'm determined to eat wholesome and healthy food, and things will start off well. But then the waiter tempts me with a sugary dessert, and without thinking about it, I accept. Then, on the way home, I'll buy a bar of chocolate. This may sound harmless, but in fact it's an addictive process.

> Addiction can be summed up by one word: MORE! We are powerless to resist MORE food, MORE sex, MORE shopping, MORE Facebook, MORE booze or MORE drugs.

There are many, many people who are addicted to sugar, and believe it or not, it can be just as deadly as drugs or alcohol. I've known of people who can sit alone in a room and binge on plastic grocery bags full of sweets until they're physically sick. Addicts always want more, and they have no idea why.

Addiction is a Loss of Control

When someone comes to me for an assessment, I often know what their problem is before they've even opened their mouth – and they'll almost certainly be in denial about their predicament. Usually, a suffering addict is incapable of uttering a single truthful statement about their habit, so I simply ask them how I can help.

I take everything they say with a pinch of salt, and then I ask them what their partner or their boss would say about their problem. That's often when things start to get uncomfortable. People typically end up in rehab because they've suffered a nasty consequence of their habit. Perhaps they've been caught being unfaithful to their partner, or they've lost their job, or they've done something silly with someone in a toilet, or crashed their car and knocked someone over.

Most addicts I've met are good people who wouldn't dream of doing such things under normal circumstances. Yet when they're under the influence of sex, alcohol, sugar or cocaine – it doesn't really matter which – they'll do things that are very bad for their own wellbeing and for the wellbeing of others.

It's usually only when the consequences of their addiction become unbearable that an addict seeks help. That moment might come when their spouse threatens to leave them, or when their boss tells them they're fired. It might come when they end up in the Accident and Emergency department at the hospital, or when a police officer wakes them up in a cell and asks, 'Do you know what you did last night?'

One addict told me that, for him, an average weekend's recreation involved five or six grams of cocaine, several bottles of champagne and two prostitutes. He'd retire to a hotel bedroom, where he'd remain from Friday night until Monday morning. Afterwards, he'd attempt to go to work as if nothing had happened. It was killing him, and I could see that just by looking at him.

His story is extreme, but his problem has elements that are common to *all* forms of addiction. It wasn't a high blood alcohol level that made him behave like that, nor was it the effect of the cocaine on his brain chemistry, or the rush of endorphins from the sleazy sex. The cause was something much deeper, and that something is what this book is about.

My own way of falling into addiction came when, as a teenager, I was feeling low and isolated. One day, I turned up early to meet someone in a pub and I ordered a pint of beer. By the time the person I was meeting arrived, I was on my second pint and it felt like a Saturn V rocket had just taken off in my head!

Suddenly the whole world was in high definition. And I could talk and make people laugh, and do all sorts of things. The anxiety and trepidation I'd been feeling on a daily basis just dissolved in the time it took to tip the beer down my throat.

But unfortunately, that's not all the alcohol dissolved. Having a drink to feel good eventually became *needing* a drink just to feel okay. A compulsion to drink more and more soon kicked in big time. I drank to celebrate *and* to commiserate. I drank when I was feeling up because I wanted to get even higher, and I drank when I was down because it was the only way I knew how to cope.

Although I didn't know it at the time, the reason I was doing this was because of the effect it had on my *feelings*.

The way that addiction affects our emotions is similar in all types of addictive behaviour – whether you're a gambler chasing the thrill of a big win or a shopaholic seeking the feeling of happiness you get from buying a nice new pair of shoes.

At the time we may think this behaviour is harmless – after all, it's natural to want to feel the best we can, so why shouldn't we indulge moderately in things that give us a little lift now and then?

In my case, the problem was that it led me into a complete meltdown. The word 'moderation' didn't exist in my vocabulary. Something within me led me to keep on drinking, even when the consequences stopped being positive and became extremely negative. I boozed constantly until I was eventually arrested for violent behaviour and sent to a psychiatric hospital.

When you're driven away in handcuffs in an ambulance, as I was, it should tell you that it's time to make a few lifestyle changes. Unfortunately, when it happened to me, I couldn't understand this, because I'd driven myself insane. I'd lost control of my actions. Why else would I have drunk vodka for breakfast every day, and repeatedly got smashed out of my head, regardless of the chaos it caused? Addiction is a loss of control. This is a common factor, regardless of what it is that we're addicted to.

An Addictive Nature

Our media almost universally portrays addicts as people who are physically dependent on drugs or booze through their own feckless choices. But in fact, an addict actually has no *choice,* because their alcohol or drug abuse is really just a symptom of a very complex emotional condition that robs them of any control.

This can surface in lots of different ways, and as a result, people can become addicted to all sorts of things: exercise, gambling, overeating, anger outbursts, computer games... In fact, when I use the word 'addict', I generally mean it to include somebody who has an *addictive nature* (even though they may never have taken illegal drugs).

This is because, as we'll see later in the book, I believe we can become addicted to almost anything with the power to alter our moods. Very few people are completely immune to this effect – all of us exist somewhere on the addictive spectrum – but for most of the population it doesn't cause serious problems.

However, for a sizable proportion of the population – perhaps as much as 10 per cent – addiction has the potential to become a serious affliction. These are the people I call 'addicts', even if they may not currently be in the throes of an active addiction. Instead, the condition might be dormant within them, and it makes them extremely susceptible to addictive processes.

During my work as a therapist at the Priory Hospital North London, I encouraged everybody on the recovery programme to call themselves an 'addict', rather than an 'alcoholic' or a 'compulsive eater'. This is because it's not the *type* of addiction that matters so much – the important thing is the *effect* it has on our feelings. Here's a typical addiction story:

Imagine that you're starting down the path to drinking too much. If you're lucky someone says, 'Don't you think you should cut down on your booze a little?' Maybe they say this before the stage when your habit becomes out-and-out alcoholism. Perhaps you're just at the *start* of a process in which you use drink to improve the way you feel. You might think to yourself, *It's true, I do drink a lot. Perhaps I should cut down*?

Now what can happen next is that whatever was causing you to drink will probably start to surface in other ways. Without further thought you might say to yourself, *Ah, I know what I need to do. I need to stop drinking, so I'll go to the gym instead.* And before you know it, you're over-exercising in an intensive bid to get the perfect body.

What you're actually doing now is continuing to try to make yourself feel better, only in a different way. If you're not careful, you'll end up becoming obsessed with going to the gym, and become addicted to excessive exercise.

As we'll see later, one reason why the medical profession finds it so hard to diagnose and treat addiction is because doctors routinely confuse physical dependency on drugs or alcohol with what I call 'true addiction' – which is something that's caused by psychological and emotional factors.

Of course, physical dependency on a substance can be very dangerous, but in the main I regard it as a symptom of addiction, rather than a cause. If you habitually use something like alcohol or nicotine, your body builds up a physical dependency on it in order to function. When you withdraw from the substance it can cause physical cravings and severe medical complications, but these can be alleviated with treatment.

However, the underlying *emotional* issue that caused the physical dependency is still likely to be present – and sooner or later it will come bubbling back to the surface like sulphur in an acidic lake.

This is the nature of true addiction: it exists in our mind and in our emotions. Being hooked on substances (like drugs or alcohol) and being addicted to behavioural processes (such as overeating or overwork) are the same thing. They're our attempts to change the way we feel.

It's interesting to note that almost all the literature published by Alcoholics Anonymous refers to alcoholism as a 'spiritual' illness rather than a physical one. It's very hard to define what spiritual means. It doesn't necessarily mean religious: it refers to something more abstract that exists somewhere in our psychology as human beings.

The implications of this are enormous because it means the medical profession is looking for a cure for addiction in the wrong place. The mainstream medical approach to treating addiction (with the notable exception of most leading private clinics) is to concentrate on breaking physical dependency, but this alone cannot solve the underlying problem.

The 'Gift' of Addiction

We know that addiction can kill. We know it can ruin the lives of addicts and those around them. We know that it destroys relationships with family and friends, and that it eats away at the very soul of an individual, wrecking their hopes and dreams.

So, it might surprise you to learn that I consider addiction to be a very special gift. This is because, during almost two decades of working as a therapist in treatment centres – patching up the carnage and misery caused by patients' destructive abuse of drink and drugs – I've never met an addict who isn't kind and generous once they're in recovery.

I've found that the overwhelming majority of addicts are extremely caring of other people. They're very sensitive and loving, and when they're sober they make good friends who are reliable and dependable. They're also capable of great creativity, and many go on to rebuild their lives through acts of charity and kindness.

I've seen addicts give up highly paid careers to become poets or artists. I know of one person who quit a highly lucrative job in order to work as a volunteer in a war zone, driving medical supplies to injured civilians.

> **When they're not under the influence of their addiction, far from being selfish and thoughtless towards their fellow human beings, the majority of addicts are extremely sensitive towards others. And this sensitivity can be a great gift.**

So, what is it that makes addicts behave in a destructive way when they're in the grip of their demons? Well, I believe that whatever we're addicted to, the answer is the same: there's an underlying part of our nature that causes us to want to alter our feelings.

The next time you're on the sofa and are tempted to reach for that extra chocolate cookie, ask yourself this question: does the feeling inside you that's making you yearn for more mean that you have an addictive nature? We'll discover the answer together over the following pages.

It's possible to become hooked on *anything* that has the power to change our moods. Whatever it is we're addicted to, the process involved is the same. The question is: what causes this universal lack of self-control?

Chapter 2

We Are Ruled by Our Emotions

Have you ever been transported back in time by a piece of music? You know the sort of thing I'm talking about: it might be a favourite pop song from your youth – or something else that has the power to overwhelm you with strong memories.

You hear it by chance and suddenly it's as if you're back in the day. You're 16 years old again, and you can literally *feel* the past come alive. Tangible emotions are stirred up – happy or sad – and all from just overhearing a simple tune.

I call this a 'Sgt. Pepper moment', because that's the one song that always triggers it for me. It reminds me of the time when, as a shy and scared teenager, I went to a record shop before going into college and bought a copy of the album *Sgt. Pepper's Lonely Hearts Club Band* by The Beatles. When I took the record into college everybody was falling over themselves to look at it because I was the first guy in town to buy it.

So there I was, sitting in the physics laboratory with this big vinyl record. I opened up the sleeve and saw a large, close-up colour picture of the four Beatles dressed in silk military-style suits – and

I felt just *fantastic*. I had the first copy of the album *everybody* wanted, and it was all mine.

This happened during the 1960s, but to this day, my memory of those feelings is still vivid, and remembering that moment fills me with emotion. Recently, I was in a record shop and I saw a CD of *Sgt. Pepper* with the original artwork on the cover – the one with the famous drum and all the faces in the crowd. You can guess what happened next: I thought, *I have to buy that!*

When I got the CD home and opened it up, I saw the same full-colour picture of The Beatles that I'd stared at all those years ago. I was overwhelmed by the memories it evoked within me. It was as if I was back in that physics lab, with my life still ahead of me. Even *thinking* about it now makes the hair stand up on the back of my neck, because it brings back every intense feeling of joy and fear I experienced as a teenager.

It's not only musical cues and photographs that have the power to do this. Similar memory-feelings can be stirred up by smells, noises, colours and events. We all experience these from time to time, and when they happen it's likely that the area of our brain called the *limbic system* is at work.

Introducing the Limbic Brain

The limbic system consists of the parts of our mind that govern our feelings and emotions, and our long-term memory. It operates by influencing something called the autonomic nervous system, which is a control network that functions independently of our conscious awareness. It's highly interlinked with the brain's pleasure centre, which plays a key role in sexual arousal, and also in the highs we feel from recreational drugs.

This area of the brain is also the part that will keep us alive in an emergency – and for this reason it has the power to override *everything* that we do. I think of it as being a bit like a flight computer on a passenger jet that's flying by the wire. When the plane's nice and steady the computer is dormant in the background – quietly monitoring everything.

But if the plane suddenly hits an air pocket or turbulence, the computer overrides the flight instructions and compensates for any sudden loss in altitude in order to stop the plane from plunging earthwards. The limbic system has a similar function in our brain when we encounter danger.

Here's a good example of the limbic system at work:

Imagine you're in a room and I'm about to throw a baseball at your head with all my strength. As the ball hurtles towards your face at great speed, your instincts tell you that when it connects it will almost certainly smash some of your teeth and facial bones.

So, what do you do? You instantly duck, and attempt to block it, of course. You do this without thinking: it's a reflex action over which you've no control. Your brain processes the information about an incoming threat and your limbic system kicks in to react in superfast time. *Bang!* It does this in order to protect you, and it happens without the need for conscious thought.

The important thing here is that your reflexes react *in a way that's beyond your control*. You probably couldn't stop yourself from ducking, even if you wanted to. It's a prime example of how our gut instincts and feelings – in this case fear of being hit by a baseball – can cause us to react in a certain way without our having any control over it.

Our limbic system has the ability to override our conscious actions, and we're powerless over its effect on us.

Remember how, in the previous chapter, we discussed the fact that addiction is all about a loss of control? Well, if our limbic system can cause us to act without control on autopilot, I believe the same process can cause the lack of control that people experience when they're addicted to something.

It explains how a heavy drinker can intend to have only one or two drinks on a night out, but then slip into downing a bucketful without thinking about it. After many years spent working with heavy drinkers, and people suffering from other forms of addiction, I'm convinced there's an overwhelmingly strong connection between the limbic system and addictive behaviour.

The Limbic Brain and Memory

Our limbic brain is capable of creating strong associations between memories and emotions. When we perceive a threat it creates powerful feelings that the brain is capable of storing away. Here's an example that illustrates this process:

Imagine you're a small child out in the street with your parents. Suddenly, a big dog comes over, and before your mother or father can intervene, the animal jumps up at you. The dog might just want to be friendly, but as you're very young, you don't know whether this creature with big teeth will hurt you or not. As far as you're concerned, it's a dangerous animal and your parents might not be close enough to protect you.

What happens next is very interesting. A part of your neurological system called the thalamus (which is the brain's telephone switchboard) takes the information about the big dog and sends it to your amygdala, the part of the limbic system that governs your feelings of fear and reward. The amygdala can react in several ways, one of which is to go: *This is a threat! FREEZE*.

If this happens, you'll be frozen to the spot with fear. And from that moment on, if you see a big dog, you'll experience an urge to freeze. If the effect is powerful enough, this may stay with you for life: some people who have an unpleasant encounter with a dog when they are very young can be afraid of the animals till the day they die.

Here's one more example of your limbic system in action:

You're walking down the street when you hear a car backfire, causing an almighty noise. The sound startles you, and it makes you physically jump out of your skin. Again, this is an involuntary act over which you've no control. You do it without thinking.

Your limbic system does many things like this, and one of its most important functions is to act like a radar warning system that's on constant alert for danger. It's a bit like a sixth sense. In fact, in my opinion, that's *exactly* what it is.

Our Sixth Sense

Our limbic system works via a whole range of feelings and emotions – we *feel* scared and we react accordingly. We *sense* that something isn't quite right. We become *aware* of danger and take evasive action.

Our brain does this by tuning in to complex nuances in our surroundings that go beyond our conscious understanding of normal visual and audible signals. When we walk into a room where other people are present, we start analyzing thousands of subtle pieces of information. Without realizing it, we're constantly monitoring body language, smells, temperature and ambience. This process is fed by our five physical senses of vision, hearing, smell, touch and taste.

I believe that when all of this data is combined in the limbic part of the brain it creates a sixth sense – our emotional ability to read a situation and translate it into feelings. This has been called many things throughout history: our *intuition*; our *instinct*; our sense of *deja vu*. It's our ability to *just know* when something doesn't feel quite right, without actually being able to explain why.

Our sixth sense is a process that operates all the time, without our knowledge, and it guides us via our feelings.

If our limbic brain has the power to override our conscious thoughts, this means we cannot easily influence how it makes us behave. The process is hardwired into our very nature as human beings. We have no control over our jump reflex when we're startled, and in the same way, an addict has no control over his or her addiction. This lack of control explains why addicts are so prone to relapse, even when they're determined to stay clean.

As a therapist, one of the things that puzzled me for many years was the way people could walk out of rehab centres having seemingly overcome their demons, only to go back to their old habits. There seemed to be no explanation for this. When patients leave a treatment centre like the Priory they're hopefully no longer *physically* dependent on substances or alcohol. In that sense they're 'clean', and when they say they'll never pick up another drink or drug they're 100 per cent committed to that.

Many addicts are intelligent, considerate people with good jobs and loving families. Yet around a third of them revert to their old behaviour when they get back into daily life. It's as if the pressure of an ordinary lifestyle is simply too much for them. They'll often resume drinking in the full knowledge of the enormous dangers involved, yet something beyond their control makes them do it. I believe what actually happens is that their limbic system kicks in and causes them to react in a way that they don't understand.

Throughout nature we see many examples of animals with highly developed limbic systems, and humans share many of these characteristics. Horses, in particular, are incredibly attuned to their surroundings, and they're very astute at reading the emotions of people and other animals. Anybody who's worked with horses will tell you that they'll instantly pick up on our moods and react accordingly. If a rider is in a bad temper, or giving off aggressive vibes, the horse will quickly become agitated too. But show a horse love and care and it will relax and cooperate.

In this respect, horses are the perfect limbic beings. They're at one with nature. We can learn a lot from them about the dynamics of addiction. In fact, for this reason, many treatment centres use equine therapy as a way of helping addicts re-connect with their feelings. At treatment centres like the Priory, therapists take a group of patients to a riding school and invite them to lead horses and ponies around obstacles.

The humans quickly learn that the horses pick up on their moods and will happily respond to positive influences, but the opposite occurs if they try to use force (I guess the old saying that you can lead a horse to water but you cannot make it drink is true!) This is something that addicts empathize with, because without knowing it, they do exactly the same.

The Dark Castle of Addiction

Addicts are *very* sensitive to other people's feelings. Yet, paradoxically, when they're in the grip of their addiction these same people are capable of being extremely selfish – I know that I certainly was when I was a heavy drinker. It's as if addicts build a dark castle to hide inside – one full of mistruths, lies, manipulation and denial.

When I was boozing I wouldn't think twice about lying to my partner if it meant I could create an opportunity to guzzle a drink. Before I knew it, I'd be telling lies on top of lies without even pausing to think. Just so I could get a sly drop of alcohol.

> There's a dark side to the limbic system that's visceral by nature. It operates beyond our conscious control and it can lead us to react to people and situations in ways that we know are bad for our long-term wellbeing.

This type of behaviour is very common, and it can be enormously hard on the family and friends of addicts, who cannot understand why their loved one (who is so kind and caring in normal circumstances) can act in such a selfish way.

How often have you heard someone say something like, 'I know it was wrong of me, but I can't help the way I feel.' You'll usually hear this when someone's done something wrong, like having a huge outburst of temper or cheating on a partner. This is interesting because it shows that our feelings and emotions – through our limbic system – can have a hold over us in ways that we don't fully appreciate or understand.

The point here is that we don't always react in a considered way: we can become a slave to our emotions. If a person tells me they've been fired from their job for smelling of alcohol, I know it's likely that they're already pretty far down the road to a very serious addiction. By the time they reach this stage they'll be weighed down by years of deceit around their drinking. This is invariably the case, regardless of their background. An important factor in understanding addiction is to acknowledge that it affects people from all walks of life.

> **Addicts come in all shapes and sizes, but their problems are always similar. It's often said in therapy circles that addiction is 'an equal opportunities illness'.**

One alcoholic I know has a photograph of himself with a group of fellow patients in a rehab centre. Among them are an affluent banker, a failed musician, a photocopier salesman, a relative of a Hollywood star, an accountant, an unemployed teenager and a retired nurse. On any given day in the Priory you'll find patients from a wide variety of backgrounds (the only common factor is that they've been lucky enough to get into private treatment).

These people suffer from a wide range of compulsive behaviours, from alcoholism and hard drugs through to food and gambling addictions. Yet in all cases their problem causes them to act in a similar way. It's as if there's something at work deep within human nature. I believe that what we're witnessing here is the limbic system misfiring and influencing us in a negative way.

I freely admit that as a violent alcoholic I lost control over my own behaviour. I simply *had* to indulge in booze or drugs, regardless of the consequences. All I can say is that my problem seemed to come from deep within me. It was visceral by nature, and it defied logical explanation.

My experience may have been extreme, but perhaps it holds an important clue for understanding our nature as human beings. In my subsequent life as a leading therapist, I've met thousands of people who've become addicted to everyday things, ranging from sex to spending. My work has led me to conclude that the urge to overindulge may be far more universal than we currently understand.

Chapter 3

Looking Beneath Addiction

When we indulge in a pleasurable activity – like a workout at the gym or buying ourselves a nice treat – something very interesting occurs within our brain. It triggers the release of natural substances called endorphins, which make us feel good. These are the body's way of perking us up, and they create a sense of contentment and wellbeing.

If you're someone who likes to exercise you'll know that after a good session in the gym you feel fit and healthy. You glow, both physically and mentally, and this is because exercise is a natural way of boosting our endorphin levels. Another natural activity that can produce this effect is laughter. When we joke and smile we feel better for it – not just while we're laughing, but afterwards too.

When we drink alcohol – or consume other addictive substances – it also triggers the release of endorphins. The booze makes us experience a change in our brain chemistry that causes us to feel more relaxed, and we may lose some of our inhibitions. For ordinary drinkers this isn't a problem. They can enjoy the buzz without going over the top; they have the self-control to avoid overindulgence.

This is a good thing, because otherwise diminishing returns set in. This happens when the benefits we get from each drink become smaller and smaller – hence the phrase 'the first drink is always the best'. If we carry on drinking, we eventually end up getting completely smashed, with all the negative baggage that entails.

So what is it that makes some drinkers able to stop before they get hopelessly drunk, while others become slaves to alcohol?

Understanding Endorphins

The word 'addict' comes from the Latin word *addictus*, which in ancient Rome was the word for a slave who was tied to a master by a debt. And just like a slave, an addict is powerless over his or her habit.

They become enslaved by a type of behaviour that involves repeated use of a substance or a process, despite suffering consequences that are increasingly negative. This pattern can occur beyond their conscious awareness, and it repeats itself, with results that get worse and worse.

Addiction is when you keep doing the same thing over and over again, regardless of the consequences, and despite the fact that it's causing harm to you or to others. If the first thing you do when you wake up in the morning is reach for a bottle of vodka, that's a pretty obvious clue that you're an alcoholic. But many, many people have drink problems that affect them in ways that are far more discreet, yet still have an extremely bad effect on their life and their health.

The drinking patterns of alcoholics vary enormously from one individual to the next. Some may drink every day, while others might go several days or even many weeks without touching a drop, only to then take part in a huge binge. The thing they have in common is that when they're in the grip of their drink problem, the rush they receive from booze – and the subsequent effect on their feelings – becomes highly addictive.

Conversely, there are some heavy drinkers who aren't necessarily alcoholics. They might drink large quantities, but the difference is that they reach a point in the evening when they decide they don't want any more, and they're able to stop. And they seem to have no problems coping with the effects of alcohol.

I've met people who can drink all day at a racecourse, yet they never actually get drunk, and when they head home they're in reasonably good shape. (I must say that these people are becoming pretty rare in my experience, but they do exist!) Such drinkers seem to instinctively know when they're reaching the tipping point and they slow down.

But an alcoholic doesn't *want* to slow down. He or she wants to find the tipping point and charge right through it. And it's not just alcoholics who behave like this. If a gambler can't resist blowing his wages, it's the mood lift from the endorphin rush of placing the bet that he's seeking.

> **Anything that boosts our endorphin levels,
> or which has the power to change our
> mood, can become addictive.**

Of course, it would be an oversimplification to say this is the only factor involved, but it's very important to understand the relationship between endorphins and addiction. However, it's clearly not the endorphins *themselves* that are the problem (otherwise we'd all be addicts, since we all create them). So there must be something else in the make-up of an addict that makes them so desperate to constantly change the way they feel.

Doughnuts and Discomfort

In order to understand addiction, we need to be aware that it isn't just the *amount* that we consume (although obviously that's an important indicator). Addiction is also characterized by the *manner* in which we behave, and the *reasons* we do it. We need to understand what drives us to self-destruct, despite the chaos and harm it causes.

Let's imagine that you're partial to the odd Krispy Kreme doughnut. Nothing wrong with that, after all they're delicious. Maybe you've had a hard day at work and you want to put your feet up and enjoy one with a cup of tea. Afterwards, you feel pleasantly full, and you spend the rest of the evening watching television before retiring for a good night's sleep.

The enjoyment you got from the sugar rush in the doughnut probably contributed to your feeling of contentment by boosting your endorphin levels, and it also changed your neurotransmitters in the brain – and you felt nice and full afterwards, too. No harm done (except, perhaps, to your waistline).

Now let's imagine a very different scenario. Let's suppose you're in the grip of a serious eating disorder and are addicted to sugary foods. One doughnut will never be enough. After the first two or three, you'll probably stop getting any real enjoyment, but still you crave more. The effect each doughnut has on your endorphin levels might be negligible by now, but still you yearn for a boost.

You feel sick and bloated, yet you carry on bingeing. Not just on doughnuts but on anything sugary you can get your hands on. Suddenly, instead of making you feel better, the bingeing is making you feel a whole lot worse. You're also worried about putting on weight, and you feel dirty and disgusting, so, in secret, you make yourself throw up.

It's a nightmare scenario, yet the next day you repeat the whole process. You start off by seeking a lift to improve the way you feel, so you reach for something sugary, and so on. However, the thing we need to tackle in order to understand why you're addicted to doughnuts isn't the *physical* way they affect you. The thing we need to discover is *why* you constantly want to change the way you *feel*.

It's the effect on your feelings that's driving the addiction, not the doughnuts themselves. The impact on your body chemistry is part of the process, but it's not the cause. It's whatever it is that's making you feel shit to begin with that's to blame.

Whatever substance or process we're addicted to, the process involved is usually the same. There's an underlying problem or issue that's causing us anxiety, and we try to alleviate it through our addiction. We may not consciously think about this anxiety; in fact, we may not even be aware of it.

These hidden feelings of discomfort can be the result of deep-rooted emotional issues that aren't always obvious, but the background anxiety they cause is always there, eating away at us.

> **If you harbour secret feelings of unease, it's only natural that you'll want to escape the distress they cause you, hence the constant craving to improve your mood by deadening down your feelings.**

The word 'disease' sums up this phenomenon very literally, because the best way I can describe addiction is to say that addicts suffer from a form of '*dis*-ease'. In other words, they're never 'at ease'. This leads them to behave in a way that's slightly out-of-kilter with much of the rest of the population. Many addicts seem to have a different way of 'doing life' to other people, and for them, this creates a vague feeling of disconnection.

The causes of these negative emotions are varied and complex, but they're not necessarily triggered by huge events. It's the constant anxiety thrown up by normal, everyday life that addicts find so hard to deal with. A recovering addict friend of mine has a phrase to describe this problem: it's not the elephants that trample you – it's the rabbits that kick you to death.

It's natural for our body to want to alleviate any distress caused by anxiety. In fact, as we saw in the previous chapter, the limbic system in our brain is programmed to evaluate any threat and take action, even when we're unaware of it. Our subconscious mind works in a very complex way, so if we secretly have issues about things like self-confidence or buried trauma, our limbic system will be highly sensitive to this.

If you suffer from '*dis*-ease' in certain situations, or in life generally, it would be logical for your limbic system to counteract this. The problem for an addict is that the way they do it is by snorting a line of cocaine, or reaching for a bottle of Scotch or by gorging on a mountain of chocolate.

In doing this, they're attempting to 'medicate' any negative feelings they might have. Addicts are usually seeking to medicate their mood in an attempt to dull down or avoid emotional pain, even when they're not aware of it.

We can only achieve long-term success in understanding addiction by tackling the causes of background anxiety and the emotional issues that I believe all addicts secretly suffer from. I'm certain of this because I've seen what happens in rehab clinics if we fail to tackle it – the patient invariably relapses.

Clearly, there's something much deeper going on than a person simply choosing to get high by snorting drugs or drinking to excess. Something compels them to keep on doing it, and as a result they develop a tolerance, which means they need to consume more and more of the same substance in order to make them feel good.

Most people who drink alcohol can probably remember the first time they drank enough to feel intoxicated. Some years down the line, they can probably drink twice as much and just feel good, rather than drunk, and that's because a tolerance has built up. But they know when to stop.

An alcoholic, on the other hand, doesn't want to stop, and as a consequence, they'll drink more and more until they're drunk. After a while, though, even constant drinking won't hit the mark, and in those circumstances they have a horrendous time just trying to feel normal. In fact, it feels like they're going insane.

Champagne or Cooking Wine: What's Your Poison?

Most people think of 'an addict' as someone who is physically dependent on drugs, but there are many other forms of addiction that can ruin lives. Similarly, the very label 'alcoholic' is confusing because for most people it summons up a stereotypical image of a homeless drunk on a park bench.

> **But in fact, it doesn't matter if someone is getting wrecked on the world's most expensive champagne in a posh nightclub or if they're glugging cheap cooking wine in an alleyway – it still has the same effect.**

A guy who lives in a £2 million mansion may feel anxious about different things to someone who lives on the streets, but the fear he feels is just the same. In my opinion they're drinking for the same reasons.

By the time an addict reaches the point of entering a treatment centre, they have the demeanour of someone who's been beaten into submission. They feel as if their life is over and they can no longer cope. Yet before they reach this point, they might still appear outwardly normal to the rest of the world; in fact, they may come across as very confident and self-assured. For every drunk in a park or junkie in a doorway there are millions of 'functioning addicts'.

Many of these addicts hold down very good jobs and they can sometimes be pillars of their communities. They are often highly intelligent and creative too. Their work life is often the last area to be affected by the consequences of their addiction – after all, they need to regularly indulge in their addiction in order to feed it, and that requires an income. If they go to work while drunk or high they won't last very long, and if they're out of a job they won't be able to buy alcohol or drugs.

If we're to solve the riddle of addiction, I believe we need to go beneath the surface to discover the real reason for an addict's dysfunctional inability to deal appropriately with their emotions. And at the very heart of this problem is the issue of sensitivity.

Every addict I've ever met seems to suffer from an oversensitivity to emotional distress. Often, they're not even aware of this – but when I talk to them, in order to get beneath the surface of their problems, I find that this is always the case.

Chapter 4

Sensitivity: Gift or Curse?

In chapter 1, I said that I believe addiction is a gift. This might seem a very strange thing to say, since it refers to a disease that causes so much harm. How can something with the potential to wreck lives be a blessing?

It's difficult to see anything positive in a condition that leads people to become slaves to their compulsions, often turning them into liars and cheats along the way. But these negative consequences, horrific as they can be, are mainly just the symptoms of addiction. I believe that at the heart of the disease lies a deep sensitivity to the stresses and strains of everyday life.

It's worth pausing here for a moment to explore this further. If we say that someone is kind and sensitive, we mean it as a compliment. We're saying that we believe they have a caring nature and that they're compassionate and mindful of the feelings of other people. I would say that this is true of the way most addicts behave when they go into recovery, and even when they're in the grip of their addictive behaviour they are still capable of flashes of great kindness.

But there's also another meaning to the word 'sensitive', and this definition is highly relevant to addicts. My dictionary defines the word sensitive as follows: *easily hurt; tender. Responsive to external stimuli or impressions. Easily offended or shocked.* It also points out that if we describe a subject or issue as being sensitive, we normally mean that it's liable to arouse controversy or *strong feelings.*

There's also a more blunt way of putting it: people with an addictive nature are simply too touchy for their own good!

I don't mean this as a criticism – I'm simply stating it as a fact. A lot of suffering alcoholics, and people with other addictive traits, will deny they're touchy until they're blue in the face. In fact, even the very suggestion that they're touchy can make them super touchy!

Exquisite Agony: Supersensitivity

I have a friend who drank heavily for 25 years. He always swore blind that he was the most easy-going man on the planet, yet he was always stomping around in a fury. He was angry and fed up at work and full of rage whenever he took to the wheel of his car. He'd also get into petty arguments and shouting matches with shop assistants.

Whenever his wife told him he was too touchy about life in general, he'd react with amazement and insist that all he wanted to do was chill out with a quiet pint. Unfortunately, he could never enjoy a 'quiet pint' because he'd invariably down eight or nine pints and wake up the next day with a steaming hangover. Which made him all the more touchy!

In my own case, I certainly know that during my drinking days I was touchy as hell. One wrong word from someone could set me off brooding for days. Even the smallest hint of criticism would be taken as a great personal slight, and I'd obsess about things that, in the grand scheme of things, were trivial. If, when I arrived home in the evening, my wife said something to me that struck the wrong chord, I'd be convinced we were on course for a huge row (this usually became a self-fulfilling prophesy).

Meanwhile, at work, if my boss spoke to me in a way that was even the slightest bit curt or clipped, I'd spend the rest of the day convinced that I'd upset him and was about to lose my job or suffer a horrendous telling-off. It never occurred to me that my boss might simply have been having a bad day himself. I was *oversensitive* to everything that he, or anybody else, said to me.

Recovering alcoholics have an expression to describe the obsessive worrying and brooding they go through – having a 'washing machine head'. This is when nagging thoughts go round and round in your mind on a constant cycle – like clothes tumbling about beyond the glass door of a washing machine.

When you're wearing your washing machine head, even the most trivial worries can drive you crazy. I once heard an alcoholic say that he felt he was the only person in the world who could go out and buy himself a brown pair of shoes and then spend the whole day worrying that he would have preferred a black pair! These worries and concerns can be about certain things, or about nothing in particular: they're really just noise, but the effect they have can be devastating.

If you find yourself constantly fretting about things that usually work out fine in the end, you could have an addictive nature. Even though the things we fret about may be trivial, the negative impact that such worrying can have on our moods and emotions can be huge. In fact, it can be extremely dangerous for our physical health and our mental wellbeing. Remember, it's not the elephants that trample us, it's the rabbits that kick us to death.

Addiction and Creativity

If you're an addict you're *super-attuned* to emotional signals. This can be a cause of distress, but it's also a gift for understanding human nature. I think it's the reason why so many addicts work in the creative spheres in life – music, literature and art. If you have the gift of sensitivity, it can be a wonderful aide to help you strive towards perfection.

The rock star Eric Clapton is a perfect example of a recovering alcoholic and drug addict who has a deep understanding of the sensitivity that binds the human race. He's a creative genius with a guitar – and when you listen to him sing *Tears From Heaven*, the song he wrote about the tragic death of his four-year-old son Conor, I defy you not to feel deeply moved. Eric can articulate things in a way that very few people can because he has the ability to connect with the feelings of his audience.

Other great names have succumbed to alcohol or drugs with tragic consequences. The British singer Amy Winehouse was clearly one of the most talented artists of her generation. Powerful emotions resonate from her lyrics in songs like 'Back to Black', in which she describes the torture of a failed relationship. You can almost feel the pain in her voice. Sadly, she died at the age of 27, after suffering long-term and well-documented problems with booze and drugs.

Whitney Houston was another rare talent who had the ability to connect with huge audiences. She died at the age of 48, after years of prolonged drug abuse. And in literature, the tortured genius is so prevalent that he or she has almost become a stereotype in the mould of Ernest Hemingway.

Sensitivity comes with a huge price for those with an addictive nature, because there's no easy way to turn it off. As we learned earlier, this is because our feelings and our emotions are rooted in our limbic system, something over which we have very little conscious control. If we're easily hurt – or as the dictionary puts it, if we're *extremely responsive to external stimuli or impressions* – then sooner or later this sensitivity is going to cause us a lot of background anxiety.

No matter how much it causes us to fret, we can't make it go away. However, we can attempt to dull it down to the point of nonexistence, and some of the ways we can do this include guzzling booze, overeating, compulsive shopping and abusing drugs. Anything, in fact, that helps to silence our washing machine head.

If this occurs at a limbic level, it might not be a conscious decision. A heavy boozer doesn't think to himself: *I've got my washing machine head on today so I'll go and get hammered in the pub.* All he knows is that he needs a drink, and that he'll feel better for getting one, at least temporarily.

As we learned earlier, in most people, the sixth sense created in the limbic system of the brain doesn't intrude on their daily lives. But in addicts it has an impact on how they feel on an hourly basis, and even moment by moment. I believe that an addict's limbic system is too sensitive, and I think this causes hypersensitivity to anxiety, which makes them feel constantly agitated and ill at ease.

If this is starting to sound a little familiar, it's because I said earlier that these feelings are just the thing that can drive us to drink or drugs.

Is Addiction in Our Genes?

The question this raises is: why do some people (i.e. addicts) seem to have a limbic system that's oversensitive to the point of being dysfunctional? Are addicts born this way, or does something trigger it? I suspect that part of the answer lies in our genes, although this is unlikely to be the only factor.

But it's worth noting that our family history undoubtedly has a huge impact on our chances of having an addictive nature. Statistics suggest that we're more likely to have an alcohol problem if a parent or a grandparent was a heavy drinker. Is this because a child who grows up around alcohol abuse is likely to copy that behaviour, or could there be something else going on?

When I talk with addicts in therapy groups I often hear things like, 'I always felt different from all the other kids when I was a child', or 'I just wanted to be like all the others, but I felt cut off.' Very often, they experienced this feeling many years before they took their first drink or drug. So could addicts somehow be genetically *different* in a way that we don't yet fully understand?

It seems that an addict's sense that 'other people have a different way of doing life' starts at an early age. It seems to pre-date any abuse of booze or drugs or sex (or whatever else they later become addicted to). Many addicts describe the feelings it created in them as 'uncomfortable' and 'disconnected'.

It's as if addicts have a predisposition from birth to be oversensitive to anxiety. They're aware of the fact that they're different from others in the way they handle emotions – which makes them feel lonely and confused. But when they pick up a drink or behave compulsively, they're no longer lonely and confused. The rush they get from their addiction temporarily boosts their confidence and deadens the awful feelings.

Often, the first thing a psychiatrist asks an alcoholic is whether or not any members of their close family are heavy drinkers. We know that many personality traits are passed on, and so it is with addictive traits.

Not everyone with a family history of drinking goes on to become an alcoholic, but the hereditary link is telling us that the problem is in some way connected to our genes. This helps to explain the feelings of being the odd one out that many alcoholics describe.

> I believe that addicts are born with a limbic system that has a genetic predisposition to be oversensitive. This doesn't necessarily mean that everybody born with this will later become an addict – but I do believe they'll inherit certain traits that make them susceptible to things that trigger addiction.

If you have an addictive nature your limbic awareness is heightened *all the time*, so you're susceptible to things that other people may be completely oblivious to. It creates anxiety even when the threat of future distress is imagined rather than real. Living with this amount of anxiety becomes untenable. We can't endure that level of stress all the time, so instead we suffer from a sort of 'limbic overload', which leads us to fall into addictive behaviour.

We don't suddenly think, *God! I can't stand this feeling. I'm going to eat eight cream cakes and then puke up!* Instead, we subconsciously seek out something that 'medicates' our inner feelings of anxiety. This 'medication' can be booze, cigarettes, drugs, shopping, sex – anything that eases our distress.

It's important to understand that even minor concerns about things that most people would regard as insignificant can cause an addict to feel insecure. Addicts are constantly on the lookout for any perceived slight. They may find even the slightest criticism very hurtful. Meanwhile they'll also be constantly seeking affirmation through praise. Some addicts do this in a very subservient way, but others can be aggressive.

An addict feels insecure even when things are going fine in their lives. They're great worriers, and they're constantly anticipating that something is about to go wrong. This fear can be far worse than the impact of the event itself when it actually happens.

Victims of sexual abuse sometimes describe how the stress of fearing their abuse will re-occur is just as painful as the feelings caused by the abuse itself. Addicts adopt a similar outlook, which is why they behave in such a self-destructive way. It's as if they think, *Fuck it, if it's all going to turn to shit anyway, I might as well go and get plastered. Get it over and done with!*

This is the point of limbic overload. The addict turns off their sensitivity by medicating it away with an addictive process or substance. This causes them to go to the opposite extreme and they become isolated and cut off from their own feelings and emotions.

I believe that all people feel a certain level of anxiety in their everyday lives – it's part of being human. The problem for addicts is that they **overreact** to these feelings, and as a result they struggle to deal with them. For example, they'll develop resentment about mere conversations, which they can play over and over again in their mind for many years. I once met a man in his late twenties who was harbouring resentment about something that had been said to him when he was four years old.

Sometimes we hide these resentments away, but without our knowledge they remain locked in our limbic system and they can easily trigger addictive behaviour. This gives us the perfect excuse to carry on using drink or drugs or whatever. Sensitivity can bring out the best in us – but it also exacts a very heavy price.

But why is this? Well, to find the answer I believe we have to go back in time, which we'll do in the next chapter.

Chapter 5

The Watchers

If you have an addictive nature, the physical state of being alive is enough to make you feel stressed. The sky may be blue and the sun shining, but you'll always be watching for something to come along and spoil things – and it can drive you nuts. I've worked with thousands of people who suffer from many different forms of addiction, but I'm convinced that the common way in which they react to life itself is always at the root of their problems.

Being human is a wonderful journey of highs and lows. We encounter things along the way that make us happy or sad, but our time on Earth is something we hopefully want to cherish. When we come up against stress or worries, there's usually an implicit belief that these feelings are caused by real events or situations.

But addicts can feel stressed and worried even when there are no external events or situations to blame. This is best described as free-floating anxiety... it's as if they're allergic to life, and they react to it differently to other people, even though they're not always aware of this fact.

If you have an addictive nature, just being on the planet means you're constantly watching for danger – and the things that you stress over are just as likely to be imaginary as they're to be real.

I believe that this state of mind – whereby you're a watcher who is always on the lookout for problems – is something that has existed within a section of the population since primeval times. It can have a powerful hold over us, and it can dominate our behaviour in ways that we don't always fully understand.

Addicts Love to Catastrophize

Imagine for a moment that you're driving a car and are suddenly flashed by a speed camera. It's a fairly ordinary event, one that takes place on the roads many thousands of times every day – but how do *you* react?

Well, let's assume you have a clean driving licence, in which case you're in no real danger of losing it over a single traffic violation. You'll probably curse under your breath and hope for the best. It might cause you a little pang of worry, followed by a few moments of unease while you mull over the possibility of receiving penalty points and a small fine. But within a short period of time – certainly within an hour or two – you've forgotten all about it. If the speeding ticket arrives in the post you'll deal with it then.

The event doesn't cause you undue emotional distress, and your response is in proportion to the experience. When the speed camera flashed, your limbic system probably kicked in to alert your brain to the possibility of a threat to your wellbeing. This made you feel uneasy, but you soon realized there was no real danger of you suffering life-changing consequences, so you were able to keep your emotions in context.

This is how the majority of the population is likely to react (the normal people, who I call the Earth dwellers!) If you have an addictive nature, however, you'll probably have reacted very differently. First of all, instead of feeling a little pang of unease when the camera flashed, you may have experienced something closer to a torrent of dread: one that went *WHOOSH!* Your limbic system would have gone into overdrive in superfast fashion and unleashed a range of complex emotions and thoughts: *Oh, my God – I'm going to lose my licence! What am I going to do?*

It doesn't matter that the maximum punishment is just a few penalty points, you suddenly find yourself convinced you're in major trouble. In your mind, you'll soon be just a whisker away from being banned from the road... and if you lose your licence, maybe you'll lose your job. Suddenly, you feel as if what started out as a minor setback now has the potential to make you penniless and destitute.

You might spend the rest of the afternoon with a feeling of dread in the pit of your stomach, while your mind continues to mull over the imaginary damage that the speed camera is going to cause to your life: *Oh my God! If I lose my job, how can I afford my mortgage?* These fears can go round and round in an addict's head like a washing machine. The thoughts they experience might be imaginary and insane, but the negative feelings they create are very real.

The emotional distress addicts feel can be triggered by the smallest things: an off-the-cuff remark by the boss, or a routine letter from the bank manager. I have a friend who once mislaid his scarf and spent the rest of the day fretting that he was worthless.

> **This type of thinking – the tendency to catastrophize any minor event in the mind – can cause an enormous amount of anxiety.**

Alternatively, it may sometimes manifest itself as a general feeling of unease, without the addict being fully aware of why they feel that way. Addicts are extremely sensitive to emotional pain – to the extent that they can catastrophize over almost anything.

But what is it that causes us to overact like this? Where does this hypersensitivity to distress come from? Well, I believe that some of us are actually hardwired by nature to behave in this way.

Fight, Flight or Freeze

If you could travel back through time to when the first humans began to walk upright on the Earth – millions of years ago – you would meet a prehistoric being called *homo erectus*. This was a primitive creature who, compared with modern humans, had very little cognitive ability and no great verbal skills.

Nonetheless, in order to survive, early humans needed to be *extremely* sensitive to their surroundings, and *very* aware of danger. They were surrounded by predators and faced extreme physical threats during every waking moment. Living in this environment must have required a highly developed limbic system: one that was always sensitive to danger in order to govern survival instincts.

If you look at the skull shape of one of our prehistoric ancestors, you'll see that instead of the upright forehead we have today, they had a head that was much flatter. In modern humans (who began to emerge much more recently), the skull shape is more rounded, and our foreheads are more pronounced at the front.

This is because we've evolved the front part of our brains – which is known as the pre-frontal cortex – in order to think our way around problems. But in our ancestors, the part of the brain that thinks logically was much smaller. Early man had very little ability to rationalize his way out of a dangerous situation. Instead, something other than logical thought helped him survive for millions of years, and that was the limbic system: the primitive part of the brain that controls our emotions and our visceral instincts.

For more than 95 per cent of mankind's time on planet Earth, our survival has depended

**on the power of our emotions to protect us,
rather than an ability to think logically.**

The pre-frontal cortex – the logical part of the brain, where our cognitive ability resides – has existed in its current form only for a relatively recent period in our history. It evolved due to our need to use tools, to communicate, and to live together in a modern society.

The limbic system is much older and much more powerful. As we saw earlier in the book, it has the ability to override other parts of the brain. For early man it was the difference between life and death, and it had the power to create strong responses.

Typically, the limbic system causes humans to react to danger in one of three ways. These are the often-quoted responses of *fight, flight* or *freeze*, which developed to ensure our survival as a species. For example, when an early human encountered a ferocious predator, he'd react by trying to fight his way out of it, or attempting to escape by running away.

Sometimes the safest thing to do would have been to simply freeze and hope the animal ignored him (most predators are attracted by movement). The speed at which he responded would have been crucial. He didn't have the luxury of time to think, so his limbic system needed to automatically take control.

These primitive survival instincts still exist within all of us, and they continue to make us sensitive to danger. If we face a serious threat, it will usually invoke a response of fight, flight or freeze.

As we know, in most of the population the limbic system doesn't have an adverse effect on daily life, but in those of us with an addictive nature it can make us react in a way that's out of all proportion to everyday events, and can leave us filled with emotional distress. I believe the reason for this lies in our ancestry.

Are You a Watcher?

An early human had three basic needs: to eat, to sleep and to procreate. Out in the wild, surrounded by predators, doing any one of these things had the potential to distract him from being aware of threats. To put it bluntly, if he was too busy making love to notice a wild beast creeping up, it would very quickly result in him being killed and eaten!

So, in addition to evolving a limbic system, early humans came together in social groups to meet the challenges they faced. Forming into small tribes was an effective survival strategy because it meant they could divide up tasks more efficiently – and they could eat, sleep and procreate in greater safety.

Within the tribe, humans began to cooperate with each other so that certain individuals could specialize in doing particular things in order to boost the collective chances of survival. For example, some members of the tribe became hunters, others raised the children, and some became skilled keepers of the fire.

Another early human characteristic that would have been highly prized for ensuring survival was the ability to stay alert to danger. Tribe members who were highly attuned to their surroundings would have been able to anticipate danger more quickly than their peers. These individuals would have needed to be extremely sensitive to noises, smells and movement. These individuals, or Watchers, as I call them, would have monitored the environment with all five senses for the subtlest signs of anything out of the ordinary that could have signalled a potential threat to the tribe.

This incoming data – sights, smells and sounds – combined in the primitive brain to create a sixth sense: instinct. It was this that helped keep humans going as a species. It was driven by raw emotions like fear and anxiety in order to trigger our responses of fight, flight or freeze.

Natural selection would have ensured that this ability was passed down through the generations. Is it possible that because of this, over the passage of time some humans evolved a limbic system that was *hypersensitiv*e?

Imagine what this would feel like: being fearful of everything, real or imagined, without respite. It would leave those affected struggling to cope with constant levels of background anxiety. They would be born worriers – those who find life itself stressful. What began as the gift of intuition would have evolved into a curse.

After many years of working in treatment centres, I'm convinced that this *is* what happened. Addictive behaviour is so automated in certain people that I believe the cause must lie, at least in part, in their DNA in the form of a 'Watcher Gene'.

> **I believe that people born with an addictive nature are the descendants of 'The Watchers'. In my view, they have a genetic predisposition towards being extremely sensitive, which makes it difficult for them to cope with emotional distress.**

Although doctors are aware that genetic factors can contribute to alcohol abuse, scientists have so far failed to discover any specific gene that's responsible. I suspect that this may well be because they're looking in the wrong place.

What they should be looking for is a gene that makes people hypersensitive to emotional distress, rather than a gene that makes them addicted to a particular substance.

If this gene exists – and I strongly believe that one day we will find it – I suspect it will be common not only to alcoholics and drug addicts, but also to people who suffer from different forms of compulsive behaviour, such as gambling or overeating. I believe that addiction is one illness, but it has many different outlets.

When Addicts Can't Cope

If you're an addict your limbic awareness is heightened all the time, so you're susceptible to things to which other people may be completely oblivious. I know a lot of alcoholics who maintain that they're always the first to sense when trouble is about to start in a pub. They can spot the early danger signals, just by being in the company of others. This isn't something that they need to concentrate on – it happens automatically.

One of my friends is a recovering alcoholic who grew up in a violent part of Essex, just outside London. He used to drink with a group of mates who regularly got into confrontations with other people, and on some occasions it was so obvious to him that a fight was about to start that he'd *feel* it in his stomach. He told me: 'I actually used to think that my mates were a bit thick because they could never see it coming, but now I realize they were just too busy enjoying themselves while I was fretting'.

There was nothing supernatural about his ability – his sixth sense was simply based on being able to correctly interpret things like other people's moods based on their body language and other subtle signals. It's an interesting thought that this drinker's sixth sense for trouble may date back to millions of years ago!

Unfortunately, for an addict, the anxiety created by all this incoming data to the brain about possible threats feels untenable. They sense that they can't cope with the constant levels of stress that it creates, so they have to go and medicate it. It's as if they suffer from a 'limbic overload', which leads them to fall into addictive behaviour.

They don't suddenly think, *Bloody hell! I can't stand this feeling. I'll go and become an alcoholic*. What they do instead is start to enjoy a substance or a behaviour that eases their inner feelings of anxiety.

This 'medication' could be booze, or cigarettes, or drugs, or shopping or sex – anything that distracts them. What happens is that they turn off their sensitivity by medicating it away. Ironically, this causes them to go to the opposite extreme and they become isolated and cut off from their feelings and emotions. In the long term this further adds to their discomfort and unease.

The Cycle of Addiction

This process begins with an addict's *hypersensitivity* to anything that might cause emotional distress. They *perceive* this to be a greater threat than it really is, and then *project* it forwards in their minds by imagining lots of horrible consequences. This can be summed up as follows:

Sensitivity = Perception = Projection

They then seek to switch off this process by numbing the sensitivity in order to gain temporary respite, but this creates a new cycle when the medicating effect wears off. Withdrawal sets in, and the painful feelings are all the more pronounced, triggering more addictive behaviour. This can be represented like this:

Painful Feelings = Addictive Behaviour = Withdrawal

which is followed by:

Withdrawal = Painful Feelings = Addictive Behaviour

which is followed by:

Addictive Behaviour = Withdrawal = Painful Feelings

Addicts go from painful feelings back to square one: more painful feelings. It's easy to see how the whole cycle of addiction then goes on to repeat itself again and again.

So, are you doomed to become an addict if you suffer from oversensitivity? In a word, no – but it does make you more at risk. Having a sensitive nature doesn't mean you'll go on to become a suffering addict. This is because some people learn to cope with the stress far better than others, while some experience events in their lives that can aggravate it. These experiences can act as triggers that tip us over the edge into active addiction. This is particularly the case in people who experience trauma during childhood, which can be highly significant. If we suffer emotional damage as a child, then, as we shall see in future chapters, being a descendant of a Watcher can quickly become a curse.

Chapter 6

Codependency – When Caring Becomes Too Much

Have you ever completely lost your temper about something while in a shop or a restaurant, only to feel foolish about it afterwards? Perhaps you were in a queue at the checkout, and someone tried to push in, making you angry? Or maybe, while you were driving your car another vehicle cut in front of you and before you knew it, you were ranting like a madman. The red mist descended and reason went out of the window.

Things like that used to happen to me all the time. Thankfully, these days I've learned to be a little more restrained when they occur, but I can still get riled at the drop of a hat if I let my emotions get the better of me.

Of course, it's perfectly reasonable to feel angry or aggrieved if someone does something that's genuinely wrong, but for addicts it goes much deeper than this. The temper outbursts we experience are often out of all proportion to the events that cause them. If this happens to you regularly, there could be something very complex going on beneath the surface of your emotions.

If you're the sort of person who has a short fuse and feels embarrassed about it afterwards – or alternatively, if you stay angry and brood about it for a long time – then this could be an important clue that you may have an addictive nature.

Emotional Outbursts

Here's a true story about something that happened to me recently which illustrates what goes on internally when addicts experience these outbursts.

I needed a mobile broadband service for my new laptop, so I visited a glitzy electrical store in London's Oxford Street. I spent ages in the shop, talking to a helpful young assistant who did his best to explain to me – while I tried to understand – all the various options. There were plenty of providers to choose from, plus short-term contracts, long-term contracts, pay-as-you-go deals.

Forty minutes later I left the store, several pounds poorer and holding a box with a computer dongle inside it. Almost as soon as I got outside, I realized that I'd bought the wrong one. But it had been a long day and I was tired, so I went home. However, the next morning, I returned to the shop as soon as it opened.

'I'd like to return this please; I've bought the wrong one,' I explained to an assistant.

The young man looked at me for a moment, and then told me that it wouldn't be possible to exchange the item or get a refund. When I asked him why not, he told me that the forms I'd filled in the previous day were legally binding. He was polite and measured, but unfortunately, that's not the way I heard it.

The way I interpreted it, he was telling me I was Stupid with a capital 'S'. I felt I should have thought about it before rushing in and signing away my rights, so I reacted like a lot of alcoholics do in similar situations: with anger.

I wondered whether the assistant would see my point of view a little better if I were to bang his head on the counter! I wasn't just angry: I was furious. When I looked at the young man I felt as if I wanted to kill him. Luckily, since giving up drinking, I'm now aware that being violent won't get me anywhere, but if this incident had happened back in the days when I was drinking heavily, it would have ended with the police being called.

Instead, this time around, I just asked the assistant for the address of his head office – albeit through gritted teeth – so that I could write to them and complain. (When I later contacted them, I didn't get a refund, but neither did I end up in a cell!)

Okay, I was miffed because I couldn't get what I wanted, but was that the only thing that caused me to feel so much anger? To some extent you might think it was reasonable for me to feel annoyed – but to the point where I felt angry enough to kill?

Well, the answer is very interesting. My behaviour was rooted in something called **codependency**, which is a condition that's likely to touch all of us from time to time. But for addicts it can be fatal.

As human beings, we depend on each other for our needs. In fact, it would be impossible for individual members of the human race to survive without cooperating with others. This applies not just to our physical needs – such as food and shelter – but also to our emotional wellbeing.

It's natural for us to want to feel valued and loved by others, and also to be capable of giving love and warmth in return. The opposite of this is loneliness and solitude, which most people would agree is a negative thing. We are social beings and in this respect we're happiest when we're in a flock or a herd, or a human tribe.

So, being interdependent and caring about others is a good thing. But what if we care **too much** about what other people think of us?

Caring can become an obsession – and that's when things start to get problematic, because it can cause us to behave in ways that have negative consequences for ourselves and other people.

Our interdependency becomes *codependency,* and we become completely reliant on others for our sense of self-worth. Caring about what other people think isn't a problem, but caring to the degree that we cause distress or harm to either ourselves or others, is.

Codependency is closely linked to addiction, and it usually develops due to the experiences we have during childhood. This is an idea that's brilliantly explained by the American therapist Pia Mellody (see the list of her works in Appendix 1 of this book).

The story I told you earlier about my experience in the electrical store is an example of codependency at work. Without my realizing it, the shop assistant was stirring up subconscious memories within me. When I was a child, I was told constantly that I was stupid, and that I always acted without thinking. That is what I felt my parents and my teacher had drummed into me: I was impulsive and I didn't listen, and this made me a bad little boy.

The knock-on effect of this is that, many years later, I'm now sensitive to any hint of criticism. If I perceive that someone is putting me down I immediately feel less than equal. The way I adapt to these feelings of low self-worth is through anger, which is a defence mechanism with the power to make me feel more than equal.

Our Implicit and Explicit Memories

These feelings of 'Less Than' and 'More Than' are very important. They help to explain why addicts behave the way they do – and they are the defining characteristics of codependency. If this all sounds a little abstract, then a simpler way to think of it is like this: if you've been through a shit time as a kid, it's no surprise if you're hyper-touchy in later life. The problem is that most of the time we have no idea it's happening.

We have two different types of memory. There are 'explicit memories', which are our normal recollections of events and experiences that we can consciously re-create in our minds. These are what we normally mean when we talk about our memories. But we also possess 'implicit memories', which are far more complex. They exist in our limbic system, but we may not actually be aware of them.

If we suffer emotional trauma as a child, the implicit memories of this can become locked in our limbic system. The result can be low self-esteem to the point where we become codependent on other people in order to validate our own self-worth. We can only feel good about ourselves through the affirmation of others, and it can cause us to behave in ways that are very manipulative and controlling in order to get what we want.

I believe that both codependency and addiction need to be understood from a limbic perspective, and that the two conditions go hand in hand. To use my earlier story again, it might be reasonable for an ordinary person to be unhappy about their treatment in a shop, but for me it went deeper. It was personal. The assistant inadvertently triggered my childhood trauma.

While it's sometimes acceptable to be upset if someone does you a wrong, if you find it goes much deeper, and it eats into your self-esteem, codependency could be at play.

If an addict's limbic system is more sensitive than most people's, it follows that we'll feel anything that happens to us more acutely, especially if it occurs during childhood when we're at our most impressionable.

Now, in lots of ways that can mean more joy, but it can also mean more fear. The highs are much higher, but the lows can be devastating, even if they are triggered by things that are seemingly minor.

Our limbic system is designed to keep us alive via *fight*, *flight* or *freeze*, so therefore it reacts to threats. If something happens to us in our childhood that we perceive as dangerous, it will kick in. It doesn't matter whether or not the danger is real or imaginary: the effect is the same.

The emotions that this reaction causes can get locked into our implicit memories, and they can remain there until the day we die if we don't do something about it. Every time the emotions are triggered they have the potential to re-invent themselves. They can also be the reason why alcoholics constantly reach for the bottle, or overeaters indulge in compulsive bingeing.

The addict doesn't consciously think about their childhood – remember, this behaviour is driven by memories that are implicit rather than explicit. Instead, more often than not, they simply find it harder to cope with the normal emotional ups and downs of everyday life that everyone encounters.

When it comes to understanding addiction, the importance of childhood experiences cannot be overstated. In fact, I would go so far as to say that childhood trauma is a predominant factor in more than 90 per cent of the cases that I've encountered during my work as a therapist.

The events that caused this trauma can range from the overt – such as forceful physical or sexual abuse – to things which, at first glance, seem to be much more minor. These can include when a parent is unaffectionate, say, or behaves in some other way that's upsetting for the child at the time.

Remember, it doesn't matter if the threat is real or imaginary, the trauma it causes has the same effect. (Pia Mellody explores this in her book *Facing Codependence*, which I recommend to anyone interested in learning more about the subject.)

Perhaps the most obvious example of childhood trauma occurs when a baby is taken from its mother. A small child is obviously completely dependent on its primary caregiver, so if it's suddenly separated from that person for whatever reason, it'll create a huge trauma. The child may go on to be adopted, and will have no conscious memory of the event, but the feelings and emotions will be locked in his or her limbic system.

That person may spend the rest of their life subconsciously trying to ease their own distress. I'll return to this point later on in the book, in the chapter about childhood trauma, but for now I shall just say that most addicts have experienced childhood issues that provide clues about their behaviour in later life.

Compulsive Helping

If you find yourself worrying about something your boss said in a meeting, that might be normal, to a degree, but if you're thinking about it over and over again, it can become unhealthy. If you spend a vast amount of time fretting about whether you've upset somebody for one reason or another, it can be a classic symptom of codependency.

One of the things you're likely to be super-sensitive about is what other people think of you, even when it's not relevant. That's codependence – the reliance or need for approval from other people.

> **In all relationships – whether it's your primary sexual relationships, your family relationships or your business relationships – if you're codependent, you can only feel okay if you know the other person feels okay about you.**

Of course, most people probably have legitimate concerns about what their boss thinks of them from time to time, but for people suffering from codependency it can be a full-time obsession. I've encountered lots of functioning addicts who are reliant on their jobs for their self-esteem.

The problem with this is that, just like every other temporary high, the boost it gives is only temporary. Addicts find themselves hanging on their boss's every word for praise or criticism, and they worry about it for hours afterwards.

Quite often we find that people who are codependent will also go around trying to fix everybody. This is called compulsive helping. Obviously, a willingness to help others is a good thing, but if it becomes controlling or manipulative then it can also become very sinister and negative.

Fundamentally, the compulsive helper is saying: 'I can only feel wanted and needed if you're okay, and if you think anything of me other than that I'm perfect, I'm going to be in a bad place.' If a codependent person can't get the affirmation they need from you, they'll be back down there again, like a scared three-year-old.

If their boss doesn't approve of what they're doing, or if their partner doesn't like what they're thinking, or if their parents question their behaviour, it sends them into free fall. If it leads them to feel 'Less Than', they have an urge to fix it.

If you have an addictive nature, you're likely to go off and start using all sorts of mood-altering substances or processes to take away the distress you feel. If you get praise or approval from your boss, that's fine, but the moment it's gone, you'll be seeking more. But no matter how much you get today, it won't fix tomorrow.

Most drunkards claim that they don't give a fuck about what other people think of them, but ask them when they're sober and it's a different story. The truth is that they often care very much. In my case, it's *why* I went in the pub in the first place. I was afraid of being criticized, and I was just waiting for somebody to tell me that I was a piece of shit. This type of insecurity drives codependency.

So, to sum up, I believe that addictive behaviour is fuelled by a chronic oversensitivity to emotional distress. These feelings exist in our limbic system and are often a direct result of childhood trauma. They can lead us to act in a manner that's beyond our conscious control, and they can lead to codependency.

In the case of somebody who suffers from an active addiction, he or she will repeatedly indulge in substances and processes in an attempt to alleviate this distress, regardless of the negative consequences. The really terrifying thing is that these influences can control almost every part of our daily lives – and as we shall see in the next few chapters, they can affect all of us to varying degrees.

Part Two
So, What's *Your* Vice?

Chapter 7

Sugar: The World's Most Addictive Substance

Most people accept that addictive substances like drugs and alcohol can kill you if you take them to excess, and for this reason, governments tend to either outlaw them (as with drugs) or at the very least ensure they're heavily licensed (as with alcohol). But there's another highly addictive substance and it probably kills more people than booze and drugs combined. Yet, most people have no idea that you can become hooked on it – and it's freely available at low cost in every supermarket and corner shop.

It might surprise you to learn that the thing I'm talking about is sugar, which I consider to be the world's most addictive substance.

If you want to get an idea of how many people are hooked on sugar, just take a walk down any high street on a busy shopping day and take a look at people's waistlines. According to UK Department of Health statistics, around a quarter of all British adults (24 per cent of men and 26 per cent of women) are classified as obese.[1]

This means they have a Body Mass Index of 30 or greater, which puts them at risk of a number of serious medical conditions. In

1993, just 13 per cent of men and 16 per cent of women were obese in the UK, so there's been a huge rise.

> **Western countries are experiencing an obesity epidemic of mammoth proportions, and the thing that's fuelling it is our insatiable desire for sugar.**

An obese man is five times more likely to develop Type 2 diabetes, three times more likely to develop cancer of the colon and two and a half times more likely to have high blood pressure (which is a major risk factor for heart disease and stroke). Obese women are 13 times more likely to develop Type 2 diabetes, four times more likely to have high blood pressure, and more than three times more likely to suffer a heart attack.

The Department of Health describes this increase in health risk as 'a significant burden' on the National Health Service (NHS). In fact, the annual cost of obesity to the NHS is officially estimated at £5.1 billion.[2]

(To put that in context, it's estimated that the cost to the NHS of alcohol abuse is at least £2.7 billion, although there's a lack of comprehensive data.[3]) It's feared that by 2050, the total cost of obesity to the UK economy will be in the region of £50 billion. Of course, none of these financial figures take into account the *human* cost of such a serious health issue.

In the USA, the obesity problem is even worse, with the Centers for Disease Control and Prevention estimating that 35.7 per cent of all adults – more than one in three – are obese.[4] This phenomenon is manifesting itself everywhere you look, and our supermarkets could now be mistaken for mountains of sugar with a roof on top.

In the past, there's been a lot of debate about the effects of a high-fat diet, but in the main I consider this to be a bit of a distraction. Of course, consuming too much saturated fat carries potential health risks, but over the last three decades, many Western societies have generally succeeded in decreasing the amount of harmful fats they consume.

Yet obesity rates remain stubbornly high in some countries, and continue to rise in others. The reason I'm so certain that sugar is to blame is because refined carbohydrates (another term for sugar) display all the hallmarks of an addictive drug in the manner in which they affect us.

They have the power to give us an instant buzz that's both pleasant and mood altering. Indeed, there have been laboratory studies done on rats which suggest that sugar affects their brain chemistry in a similar way to cocaine.

The Crack Cocaine of Comfort Eating

You don't need a scientist to tell you that food, one of our basic human needs, can also be extremely seductive. When we eat it creates pleasant sensations that can change our moods. Anything that's packed with refined carbohydrates – such as cakes, chocolate, and any foodstuff containing processed white flour – will cause an instant release of energy that has the power to give us a strong lift.

When we consume refined carbohydrates it accelerates the absorption of an amino acid that our brain converts to serotonin, a powerful neurotransmitter that makes us feel good. It's a similar process to what happens when you drink alcohol that gives you a buzz – you feel fantastic and you want to keep it that way. There's really no difference between that and when you eat a bowl of ice cream or drink a glass of cola.

If we eat to the point where we're full, it also creates a feeling of satiety, which can be very pleasant and dreamy. It can make us feel positively lethargic. I'm sure you know the sort of feeling I'm describing: it's as if Christmas lunch is all finished, the fire is roaring away, and we're dozing off in front of the TV without a care in the world.

So, if you're feeling down, or ill at ease, it doesn't take much to work out that comfort eating is an instant way of giving yourself a lift: and sugar is the crack cocaine of comfort eating. It's for this reason that when a patient is admitted to an addiction programme at an enlightened treatment centre, one of the things therapists prohibit them from doing is keeping any chocolates or sweets in their rooms on the ward.

> **Food can become an addiction just like any other. The benefits to our mood decrease with the amount we eat – until eventually the consequences become extremely negative, as we continue to repeat the behaviour.**

If this sounds a little crazy, let's try comparing the effects of refined carbohydrates to another addictive substance – alcohol:

When an alcoholic is feeling down, they'll take a drink in order to give themselves a lift, either consciously or subconsciously.

The same can be said for sugar. When we binge on refined carbohydrates we consume way beyond a healthy calorie intake, and the reason we're doing it is to change the way we feel.

Alcohol is a substance that a large proportion of the adult population overindulges in, to the point where it causes them serious health problems.

This can be said of sugar, too. In fact, if you accept the official NHS statistics in the UK, the negative cost of obesity to the nation's health is far higher than the cost for booze.

Alcoholics seem to have no control over the amount they drink, regardless of the negative consequences.

It's the same with sugar. No rational person wants to overeat to the point where they become morbidly obese, yet there are people all around us who cannot help themselves from doing exactly that.

Alcohol causes people to behave in a way that's harmful to themselves and to others. They consume more and more, with diminishing returns to their welfare.

The same applies to sugar. It might not be as overt at first glance, because the effects creep up more slowly, but I've seen many lives ruined by the misery caused by compulsive eating. In fact, I estimate that in rehab units today, we treat as many women for eating disorders as we do for alcoholism.

An alcoholic wakes up in the morning and thinks: *I feel like crap because I drank too much last night. I'm a piece of shit.*

The same applies to sugar. A compulsive eater wakes up in the morning and thinks: *I feel like crap: I ate too much last night. I'm a piece of shit.*

The Pain of Overeating

Yet, despite all the evidence, I regularly come into contact with people who seem to pooh-pooh food addiction – they think it's not a genuine phenomenon. I suspect this is because food addicts don't always implode in dramatic circumstances like alcoholics or junkies are inclined to do.

If a drunkard crashes his or her car the consequences are instant and noticeable. For food addicts the effects build up more slowly, but they eventually reach a low point that's just as painful in its emotional impact. Food addicts go through a rock bottom just like other addicts – the only difference is that it's not as obvious to the outside world.

For example, if a cocaine addict spends four days holed up with hookers in a hotel room, that's an obvious meltdown. But someone with food addiction will come more quietly to a state where they can't cope with life anymore. As their weight increases, their self-esteem falls and they feel worthless and unable to face the world.

It's important to note that in addition to overeating, food addiction can also trigger related eating disorders such as bulimia and anorexia (which we'll look at in a later chapter).

While obesity affects men and women in roughly equal numbers, it tends to be women who seek help in greater numbers for food addiction. Certainly, the emotional impact seems to be more overt for women. There's an expectation in society that a woman should be a certain size or shape. Skinny women tend to be revered and held up as fashion idols, whereas the opposite is normally true for women who are overweight.

If somebody has low self-esteem, this creates a vicious circle. They comfort eat in order to alleviate their emotional distress, but this causes weight gain, which in turn lowers their self-esteem even further. So what do they do? They comfort eat even more.

Sometimes this process can be going on in the background for many years, and it can be linked to all sorts of emotional pressures or issues. A friend of mine is a recovering alcoholic who spent years boozing every night while his charming wife sat alone at home. All that time she was overweight, and she tried every diet under the sun in order to slim down. It made her desperately unhappy, but she just couldn't shift the weight. But when her husband gave up drinking, the pounds suddenly fell off of her.

It didn't take me long to work out what had been going on in their marriage. While my pal was out getting plastered, his wife was at home comfort eating because she was lonely and miserable. But when her marriage improved, because he gave up drinking, her self-esteem grew and her eating habits became healthier.

The fact that being severely overweight is usually linked to emotional problems is an extremely interesting point – and it has profound implications for the diet industry. People often overeat because an emotional issue in their lives is causing them distress. They're trying to alleviate this discomfort through food.

This probably explains why almost every diet plan fails to be successful in the long term. How many times have you heard somebody say that they lost weight through a certain type of diet, but as soon as they stopped they put it all back on again?

Of course it's possible to physically slim down if we limit our calorie intake, but if the emotional issues that caused us to overeat are still present, it's no surprise that the pounds soon pile on again once we go back to our usual behaviour.

Most of us probably eat too much from time to time, just as lots of people who aren't alcoholics occasionally get drunk. But for some people food can become a compulsion. If you find yourself regularly feeling guilty about eating too much chocolate, or sugary snacks, then it might be time to ask yourself why you continue to do something that's ultimately making you unhappy.

> **If you're a little overweight, but it doesn't affect your self-esteem, you probably don't have too much to worry about. But if you're obese and it's affecting your health – and causing you to be unhappy about the way you look – I'd suggest that your problem is almost certainly rooted in emotional issues.**

There's some evidence that obesity tends to affect people on lower incomes the most. It seems the poorer we are, the poorer our diet (although that's not to say there aren't plenty of wealthy people who are obese). But people on low incomes often experience other issues in their lives that make them unhappy.

There are lots of cheap, healthy alternatives to sugary foods, but this doesn't seem to make any difference. In almost every case of food addiction that I've encountered, the behaviour is caused by emotional issues, which are either triggered by problems in childhood or occasionally by some traumatic event in later life.

Our issues around food often begin at a very early age. It doesn't surprise me to learn that the official figures for obesity confirm this to be the case. According to UK Department of Health statistics, nearly one in 10 (9.4 per cent) of pupils in primary school reception classes (i.e. kids aged 4–5 years) are obese.[5] By the time they reach Year 6 (aged 10–11) this figure has risen to nearly one in five (19 per cent).

I believe that one of the contributory factors is that parents are overweight themselves and children are taught they're good if they eat up all their food. Instead of encouraging kids to 'eat until you're full', we tell them they're a good boy or a good girl if they clear their plates. Some of this is no doubt learned behaviour from previous generations who went through austerity during times of war, but that's only part of the picture.

If we're given love and affirmation, and told that we're good for eating up all our food, it boosts our self-esteem and makes us feel better about ourselves. While this pattern won't necessarily create a food addiction on its own, it does establish a link between food and self-esteem at an early age, which can cause problems in later life.

Food Can Alter Our Moods

If you're a person with an addictive nature, food automatically has the potential to be a mood-altering substance with addictive properties. When you eat well you feel better about yourself – so if you're feeling low it feels natural for your body to crave more food.

I know that I certainly find it hard to resist a croissant or two, and there are plenty of occasions when I eat far too much. This is something that's very common among recovering addicts. If you watch somebody as they start to recover from an addiction, very often you'll notice that they start to put on weight.

There are lots of self-help groups for addicts, and if you ever attend one you'll probably see plenty of caffeine and sugar being consumed. This is because people often substitute one addictive substance for another.

The early literature on addiction, which was written in the first half of the 20th century, actively encouraged alcoholics to use sweets and chocolates as a way of combatting booze cravings. This isn't an approach I would recommend, since it's really just papering over the cracks and transferring one addictive process to another, but it clearly illustrates the powerful effect of refined carbohydrates.

The adverse effects of refined carbohydrates have been very well documented in the USA by an accomplished author called Gary Taubes. In his book, *Good Calories, Bad Calories: Fats, Carbs, and the Controversial Science of Diet and Health* (published as *The Diet Delusion* in the UK), Taubes argues that refined carbohydrates contribute to a range of health problems.

I fully agree with him. The use of high fructose corn syrup – a very powerful refined carbohydrate – is widespread in the USA. This substance is not only very sweet, but also it's said to switch off an enzyme in the liver that normally tells the body it's full. So it's little wonder some people have trouble limiting their calorie intake.

If anyone still has any doubts about the addictive nature of sugar, all they need to do is look at the effect it has had on human history. There were two products above all others that powered the transatlantic slave trade – one was nicotine in the form of tobacco, and the other was refined carbohydrates, as produced on sugar plantations.

Anything with a demand strong enough that humans will enslave each other in order to satisfy the craving it creates is definitely addictive in my view. For this reason, when treating obesity, we need to stop concentrating purely on the physical causes (i.e. too much food), and start looking for the emotional reasons why people overeat.

Chapter 8

How Many Times Did You Check Facebook Today?

Are you one of those people who can't resist checking your Facebook page, no matter where you are and what else you're doing? How often do you log on? Once a day, twice a day, or every 20 minutes? Perhaps you constantly peek at Facebook while you're at work, even if you know your employer doesn't like it? Well, you certainly aren't alone.

The founder of Facebook, Mark Zuckerberg, has revealed that his social networking platform now has more than a billion registered users around the globe.[6] Yet a decade ago, in December 2004, Facebook had just 1 million users. So how has it managed to grow so rapidly that it's increased its size a thousand times over?

Clearly, whatever Facebook offers, a lot of people want it. Many of us are unable to resist our fix of gossip from friends and family, and where's the harm in that? Well, the answer depends on the effect it has on you.

Has being on Facebook ever caused you to have a row with your partner, or led to embarrassment at work? Have you ever forgotten to do something important because you were too busy updating your status; or have you ever woken up exhausted because you've been up half the night on the internet? Do you worry or obsess about things that you or other people have said on Facebook?

In 2008, I caused a bit of a media storm when I argued that people were becoming hooked on the urge to acquire more and more friends on Facebook in order to appear popular and successful. I warned that women were particularly vulnerable, as they often get their self-esteem from relationships. My comments raised a lot of eyebrows at the time, but today most rehab clinics are coming round to the idea that social networking sites can have an adverse effect on people with an addictive nature. Of course they do have a role to play in modern life as a communication tool, and I currently use Facebook myself in this way.

So, what is it about social networking that we find so seductive? Well, there are potentially several complex emotional processes at play.

> **When we log on to Facebook, and we see that we have lots of friends, it gives us affirmation that we're valued. We feel popular and liked, and this boosts our self-esteem. It gives us a little buzz and we feel better about ourselves, and this can be very addictive.**

In my opinion, nobody is completely immune to this effect, which might explain why Facebook is so universally popular. If you're a well-balanced individual and you're confident of your own self-worth, then it's not going to cause you too many problems.

But what if you suffer from low self-esteem? You find yourself constantly bombarded with messages from all these friends who seem to have wonderful lives, and who are always having such a great time. Pretty soon, you're going to start feeling 'Less Than'. Why aren't *you* having the same brilliant fun as them? There's a danger you'll become insecure, which in turn will make you crave affirmation all the more.

Of course, there's nothing evil about the idea of Facebook in itself. Keeping in touch with others is a natural thing to do. The problem for addicts is that it can create an altered reality in which everybody *seems* to be having a wonderful time, even when their life is a pile of shit! It creates an expectation that everything ought to be hunky-dory *all* the time – and when it's not it creates a huge dent in our confidence.

Facebook is a very superficial way of interacting with others. It's like a TV picture of our lives, and in my opinion, it shows how we've become obsessed with 'the Culture of Celebrity'. When Andy Warhol said that in the future everybody would be famous for 15 minutes, he underestimated it, because he couldn't have foreseen Facebook.

Today, everybody wants to be famous – all the time – all over Facebook, forever. The way people portray themselves on their page is exactly as if they're a mini celebrity. Their every waking moment becomes part of a living soap opera, no matter how mundane the detail might be. Facebook is the ultimate reality show (the irony being that the reality it portrays is built on foundations that are false).

On Facebook, people live in a world that's sugar-coated and packed with fun. Of course, we all know that the real world is very different. Genuine celebrities (who, after all, are just normal human beings themselves) are often the first to admit that their glittering public persona is a myth. They suffer the same stresses and strains as the rest of us. It's called being human...

The Man with 5,000 'Friends'

So let's look in a bit more detail at what happens when a person with an addictive nature repeatedly checks their Facebook page. Why do they do it? Well, at a subconscious level, they could be searching for reassurance about their self-worth. They look at all those friends, and think that they must be popular.

This might sound harmless, but their hopes are rarely validated, and the more they find themselves searching, the more likely it is that they have issues about their self-confidence, hence the need for constant affirmation. I've encountered young women who panic if they can't check Facebook, yet they go into meltdown when they do because everyone seems to be doing so much better than them.

In fact, if you want to feel bad, just go online and see how many more friends everyone else has. Yet the very idea of counting our friends in order to evaluate our self-worth is slightly preposterous. I saw one person on Facebook with almost 5,000 friends (the level at which I'm told many accounts are capped). I don't think I even *know* 5,000 people, let alone have that many friends!

Modern technology allows everybody to be connected 24 hours a day, with no respite. We're bombarded with emails, texts, phone calls, tweets and Facebook messages. This might seem a great idea, but like most things that we enjoy to begin with, diminishing returns soon begin to set in, and the consequences can be increasingly negative.

The limitless connectivity that technology facilitates can become an addictive process in itself.

I know that when I'm in a restaurant I sit there constantly checking my phone for messages. It almost becomes a reflex action that's beyond my control. If I don't do it, I start to worry. What if somebody is trying to get hold of me? Am I missing something important? Is everything else okay in the rest of the world? It's not a nice feeling.

Here's a little test you might like to take. Try switching your phone off for a whole day and see what sort of effect it has on you. Ask yourself:

⇨ Are you able to enjoy the peace and quiet?

⇨ Or do you feel anxiety starting to creep in?

⇨ Do you start to feel uneasy about being out of touch?

⇨ Do you get a vague sick feeling in your stomach that simply won't go away until you reconnect with the rest of the world?

In other words, do you feel anxious and uneasy when you stop using your phone as an emotional crutch? These are the classic symptoms of withdrawal.

Mobile Devices and Anxiety

I have a friend who is a recovering alcoholic and he simply *has* to take his BlackBerry with him everywhere, including on holiday. Even when he's by the pool in a hot country, he forces himself to check it at periodic times during the day, regardless of whether or not he's actually expecting any messages.

So, instead of relaxing and enjoying his holiday, his mind is always wandering back to concerns about work and other minor issues at home. He can actually *feel* a small amount of tension building up in his stomach before he checks his phone, and then he experiences a little wave of relief if everything is clear and there are no troublesome emails. On the rare occasions that he actually gets a message, he's straight back into work mode and projecting about what's going to happen when he returns to the UK.

The procedure my friend goes through by constantly checking his BlackBerry is part of an addictive process, and it's caused by the background anxiety about life that most addicts suffer from. When he picks up the phone he's seeking to alleviate that anxiety by reassuring himself that there's nothing bad going on back home. When he gets affirmation of this, it temporarily relieves the anxiety, and reassures him that he's okay.

Unfortunately, the respite is temporary and diminishing returns set in, causing him to spend the whole holiday worrying about work. This makes him all the more stressed, which makes him even more of a slave to his BlackBerry! The process he goes through is beyond his control because it's triggered by his limbic system and is a symptom of codependency. He's always on the lookout for a threat: and his BlackBerry is his warning system.

> **If you're a slave to Facebook or your mobile device, it could be a sign of deep insecurity, which can be a major cause of addiction.**

It might not seem like an addiction **per se,** but the process is the same as if you take drugs or drink booze. You do it again and again, looking for an instant lift. The way to tell if you have a problem is by examining the effect that it has on your life. If it's causing negative consequences, you need to ask yourself **why** you're doing it.

One of the reasons that modern technology causes so many issues for people with an addictive nature is that it's omnipresent: there's no respite in our daily lives from the 24/7 chatter of the rest of the world.

Another problem is that it can dehumanize the interaction between people. I've given talks and lectures in schools, and one of the things pupils constantly tell me about is the number of problems and fights that are caused by things that have been posted on social networking sites. It's easy when you're sat in front of a computer screen, or tapping on a phone, to write something nasty and offensive about someone that you wouldn't dream of saying to their face.

We now regularly see items in the news about people who've been arrested for this kind of thing; it's known as 'trolling', but it's just bullying under a different name.

There are at least two major ways that mobile technology can affect those with an addictive nature. On the one hand it becomes a conduit for channelling their fears and anxiety: they need to keep checking their emails or messages to reassure themselves that nothing bad is going on that they need to know about.

The second effect is that it allows their codependency to run riot. If we're codependent we're reliant on other people to validate our sense of self-worth. We don't feel okay unless we're certain that others feel okay about *us*. This means we're always worried about what other people think of us – and it can feel like torture if, as a result, we find ourselves worrying about the finer semantics of every email or text message we receive.

This is something that people with an addictive nature find themselves doing all the time. An email can be read in many different ways, depending on its context. If you find yourself worrying about every little word and phrase that your boss uses in an email, this could be a sign of insecurity on your part.

Perhaps you've sent an email and then found yourself worried about how it will be interpreted? Was the tone too curt, or will the recipient mistake what you meant for something else? Were you too familiar, or too gushing? These are all classic signs of the sort of 'people-pleasing' behaviour that can be a symptom of codependency.

When patients are admitted to treatment centres like the Priory, one of the first things the nurses do is take away their phones. This is because patients need peace and quiet, and it's beneficial for them to be cut off from the temptations of the outside world.

When I counsel alcoholics and addicts who are in early recovery, I usually advise them to avoid using Facebook because I've seen first-hand the negative effect it can have on people when they're in a delicate state.

If recovering addicts whose lives are in tatters log on and see a picture of a friend on holiday in the Caribbean, or driving a brand new car, the effect on their emotions can be devastating as it reinforces feelings of 'Less Than'.

The emotional impact on women, in particular, can be very powerful, especially if they suffer from low self-esteem. If, for example, a woman is recovering from a food addiction and she goes online and sees lots of super-skinny women having a great time, there's a danger she'll compare herself in a negative light. If this happens it can trigger a food binge and the whole addictive process starts once again.

Addicts can become very obsessive in their behaviour – and there's no doubt that for some people, the need to check Facebook or reach for their mobile phone to check messages becomes a compulsion. In the case of my friend and his BlackBerry on holiday, I'd say it borders on becoming an Obsessive Compulsive Disorder (OCD).

There are lots of words that are used to describe addiction, and one of them is 'compulsivity'. So if you find yourself 'compelled' to check Facebook all the time, you might need to ask yourself why.

Another area in which modern technology impacts on addiction is through computer gaming. Rehab centres are starting to see more and more cases of young men, and in particular teenage boys, who become addicted to playing immersive computer games.

In real life, these people are often shy and lacking in confidence, but in the digital world they become masters of their own universe. They end up playing obsessively for hours on end, neglecting to eat or sleep, and sustaining themselves through the use of drugs to keep them going. It's a destructive downward spiral.

Chapter 9

Do You Shop Till You Drop?

Have you ever bought an item of clothing that looked irresistible in the window of a store, only to find that you never actually wear it after you've taken it home? It stays in the wardrobe untouched, while you wait for a suitable occasion to put it on. Meanwhile, within days, you're off shopping again, on the lookout for something new.

We've probably all done something like this from time to time. Not just with clothes, but with all sorts of material goods. I know people who've bought cars on impulse. Buying things that we don't really need is a fairly common behaviour. I've met lots of women who've spent hundreds of pounds on shoes that they've never even taken out of the box. Similarly, there are plenty of guys who've splurged on expensive gadgets that end up in a cupboard, gathering dust.

So why do we do it? Well, typically, one reason might be that the acquisition of desirable things can have a powerful effect on our feelings. We all know that when we buy something we adore, it can give us a bit of a lift.

The problem is that the fix that shopping provides is a temporary one – and it can land some people with a whole lot more problems than it solves.

How often have you heard yourself, or someone else, say something along the lines of: 'I was feeling a bit down so I treated myself to a new outfit to cheer myself up.' I'm certainly partial to a bit of 'retail therapy' myself. In fact, I sometimes joke that there's no problem in the world that can't be fixed by a trip to Selfridges in London's Oxford Street or Macy's on 5th Avenue, New York.

Let's suppose I'm feeling a bit down. I might find myself in an expensive boutique, gazing longingly at designer clothes by Dior Homme. I imagine how great one of those slick black outfits would make me look, if only I could afford one. Of course, the reality is that I almost certainly don't *need* a new suit, or a new shirt and tie. It's not the goods themselves that I want: it's the way they make me *feel...*

It's my perception that the designer clothes will make me look good in front of other people. So the real reason I want to buy them is because there's something going on deep inside of me, and it makes me crave a temporary lift. I want to buy the clothes in order to boost my self-esteem. If I'm feeling 'Less Than', like most addicts do on a regular basis, the acquisition of a great new outfit seems like the perfect pick-me-up.

The Thrill That Always Fades

I've heard a lot of people casually say that they're addicted to shopping, but they phrase it in such a way as to suggest they regard it as a bit of a joke. It's often portrayed as something harmless that's caused by well-intentioned over-exuberance. It's almost like a badge of honour – that we have the ability to '*shop till we drop*'.

A lot of folklore has grown up around the shopping experience – you only have to open up a newspaper or a glossy magazine to be bombarded by it. As a society we've built giant indoor arcades that serve as retail cathedrals, and it's possible to lose ourselves inside them for hours on end. If we're feeling low, or looking to escape the mundanity of daily life, they're the perfect distraction. Everything glitters and the choice is endless.

Buying things might be perfectly fine if you can afford it – and it doesn't have any negative effects on your life – but if you're doing it to fix your feelings then pretty soon diminishing returns are likely to set in. That's when the problems are going to start.

There's a saying in rehab circles that for an addict, if buying one thing is okay, then buying one in every colour has to be even better. In the same way that alcoholics use booze to medicate themselves in order to alleviate their distress, shopping can become a powerful compulsion for someone with an addictive nature.

> **The anticipation of the acquisition of an item – and the ritual that surrounds the purchase itself – triggers a response in the brain that temporarily raises our mood.**

You buy the new shoes and you get the thrill of a buzz, but from the moment you leave the store they cease to have the same effect. You might get a bit of a thrill the first time you wear them, but sometimes you don't even bother to put them on again. Instead, what happens is the next time you feel down you move on to the next phase of acquisition – and start hunting down your next purchase.

The fix is only ever a temporary one, so you keep repeating the behaviour. Eventually, you find that all your credit cards are maxed out and you've no money to pay the bills. So you feel even lower – which in turn makes you crave a spending lift. It's the classic circle of addiction, in which a compulsive process is repeated over and over again with consequences that are increasingly negative.

The reason the benefits are only temporary is that it's mainly the act *of acquisition* – the buying transaction itself – that provides the thrill. Owning the goods might boost our self-esteem, but the initial high is the bit that has the potential to be the most addictive.

It's the same feeling that gamblers experience at the precise moment they place a bet. It's not winning that gamblers become addicted to (after all, almost every compulsive gambler ends up losing everything), it's the thrill and anticipation of placing the bet, and the thought that they *might* win.

I've worked with many individuals who are just as powerless over their spending as they are over their consumption of booze or other substances. Very few addicts have only one outlet for their problems, so what tends to happen is that compulsive shopping goes hand in hand with other addictive processes. And it affects both men and women.

Let's say you feel like shit because you've got a steaming hangover and you disgraced yourself in front of your workmates in a bar last night, or you upset your partner by coming home late. Typically, you might go out and buy something nice to make yourself feel better. You might also decide to lavish a load of cash on an expensive gift for your partner, as a way of winning back their affection.

A friend of mine, an alcoholic, would buy his wife an expensive gift after every occasion he went on a wild bender. She ended up with a wardrobe full of Gucci and Chanel handbags, but still had a miserable life because her husband was never around.

Of course, not everybody who treats themselves to something nice is a compulsive shopper, but the mountains of personal debt we're sitting on in the UK and USA suggest that far too many of us are going in for retail therapy. In Britain, research by the debt charity Citizen's Advice shows that 10 per cent of us are struggling to pay off amounts of £30,000 or more, not including mortgage debt. Collectively in the UK, we owe around £1.43 *trillion*.[7] And the situation in the USA is even worse. These vast levels of personal debt can play havoc with our relationships and cause our lives to spiral out of control.

Chasing the Celebrity Myth

In my opinion, many of the debt problems we're facing are fuelled by the Culture of Celebrity, which I mentioned in the last chapter. It seems that just about everybody wants to look like their favourite celebrity icon – whether it's David Beckham or Kate Moss – or even the cast members of popular reality TV shows like *Keeping up with the Kardashians* or *The Only Way Is Essex* (the latter have inspired a whole new style in the UK that celebrates fake tans and uber-grooming to a ridiculous level).

This desire to emulate celebrities permeates all levels of society and has been going on for generations. Before the advent of TV, people looked to royalty for inspiration on what to wear. Even today, when the Duchess of Cambridge wears an outfit it sells out within hours of her being seen in it.

Millions of us flock to the high street in search of fulfilling a dream to be like the rich and famous, and the manufacturers of goods respond by investing millions in making their products look desirable. After all, if I own a pair of sports shoes with a cool label then I must be doing okay! Of course, this often turns out to be a myth.

> The subliminal message is simple: if you want to be okay, you have to wear the right clothes, or own the right phone or tablet computer.

In many ways we've come to define ourselves through the aspirational brands that we acquire for ourselves. This leads to absurd situations where the demand for certain products actually goes up if their price *increases*. Economists have a phrase for these products: they call them *superior goods*. The whole point of purchasing them is that they're expensive – the buyers are hoping that a little bit of glamour will rub off on them.

If you buy a designer handbag or a man's tie from Louis Vuitton you expect it to be beautifully crafted and of high quality – but it's also the expensive label itself that many people crave. It makes a statement of wealth: and you're telling the world that you must be okay if you can afford the best.

The flipside of the desire to look good is the fear we have of looking impoverished in front of others. So we buy things, especially clothes, and then never wear them because we're saving them 'for best'. We worry that we'll have nothing decent to wear if we have to attend an important event, and this insecurity can lead us to hoard things for some mythical future occasion. It's probably sensible to have something smart to wear when we need it, but if we suffer from insecurity about life in general, this can lead to compulsive behaviour.

When Buying Becomes an Obsession

When I first got sober, I nearly bankrupted myself by becoming obsessive about clothes. My wardrobe at that time was poor, because when I was drinking I didn't care about my appearance, all I cared about was booze. When I stopped though, I thought it would be nice to have some decent things to wear. But things got out of hand. I discovered charity shops and my ex-wife and I would spend our days off looking for outfits. The concept of charity shops was fairly new at the time so there were some good bargains, including designer clothes at very low prices.

I ended up with a bedroom of my own with four double wardrobes in it, packed full of clothes I'd bought in charity shops. All the suits, shirts and trousers were crisply ironed and colour-coordinated, but the problem was, whenever I looked in a wardrobe I'd ask myself, *Shall I wear that today?*, and then, *Ah, but what if I want to wear it tomorrow?* So in the end I'd just wear the same T-shirt and jeans I'd worn the day before.

All those great clothes were just stuck there – they were no use to me whatsoever. It sounds crazy, but I can assure you it happened!

I've come across similar behaviour in fellow addicts many times. I've met women who've spent a fortune on baby clothes, even though they've no children of their own, and in some cases aren't even in a relationship. There's no prospect of the baby outfits being used in the near future, yet they still continue to buy them.

I have a friend who became obsessed with owning the latest Mercedes sports car. He splurged on a brand-new silver convertible, and it made him feel great for a while, but he then spent the next three years wishing he'd bought the same model in black! Eventually he ended up in rehab (for problems with booze). He's now in recovery and the proud owner of a second-hand saloon car – and he's much happier.

If we're insecure and suffer from low self-esteem, there's a danger we can come to rely on material possessions for our prestige.

Back in the days when I was a heavy drinker, and working as a salesman, I was obsessed with driving the right type of car. This is something I see today in people with an addictive nature. The family finances might be in a terrible state, but the main breadwinner will insist on having an expensive car like a BMW 3 Series. It's their way of trying to tell the world that they're okay.

For me, a car was always a matter of prestige. I can distinctly remember that, as a salesman, any self-esteem I felt came from the model of company car I had. When I was given a BMW 320 I thought that I'd arrived in the world; it didn't matter that I wasn't paid very much. Later on, I was upgraded to a Range Rover and I felt even better.

I felt that my self-worth as a human being was defined by the size of the car I drove, instead of the sort of person I was.

One day my boss gave another member of staff a humble Austin Allegro when his vehicle was up for renewal. I remember thinking,

If he comes to me and says I can have an Allegro I'll tell him to stick his job up his backside. I cared more about the car than I did about my overall financial wellbeing.

Are You a Compulsive Shopper?

So, how can you tell if your shopping habits are compulsive? Well, there's nothing wrong with spending money on things you like, but it depends on the **reason** you're doing it, and the **effect** that it has on you. If you've lots of things at home that you've bought but never used, that's an obvious clue. You can't have needed them if you've never used them – so there must be some other reason for the purchase.

If you were doing it as a sticking plaster for negative feelings, or in order to boost your self-worth, then it might be a sign that you have an addictive nature. My own example of having four wardrobes full of unworn clothes was an extreme one, but it probably bears more similarity to the way many people behave than you might think.

We're all partial to the thrill of acquisition, and for many people it's harmless, just as booze is harmless for those who are able to consume it sensibly. But for some of us, acquisition becomes a compulsion.

When you think about it, a lot of hobbies are based around the innocuous thrill of collecting things like stamps or coins. It's the **acquisition** of these items that gives us pleasure. To some extent you could argue that all hobbies are about distracting us from the problems of everyday life. They help us relax – that's the whole point of them.

Here's a very simple test to discover whether or not you're susceptible to compulsive spending. The next time you're out at the shops, or browsing Ebay or Amazon at home, and you spot something that's simply irresistible, pause for a moment to ask yourself if you really *need* it? Take a breather for an hour and walk round the rest of the shops, or log off from your computer for a while if you're shopping from home.

If you still want to make the purchase after that – and more importantly, you think you can afford it – then go ahead and buy it. But you'll be surprised how often you change your mind. I've tried this many times myself, and usually I don't purchase the item.

Shopping might seem low on the addictive spectrum, but that doesn't mean it's not capable of ruining lives. If you run up huge debts, and it drives you into further problems with other addictive processes, the consequences can be huge.

Thankfully, there are some very good self-help organizations for those with these problems. You can find details of them in Appendix 2 of this book. In the meantime, feel free to try out my little test the next time you're shopping...

Chapter 10

Confessions of a Workaholic

Have you ever been so busy at work that you skipped lunch? Maybe you made do with a packet of peanuts at your desk, and a sour coffee from the vending machine – in which case you probably felt pretty crap by the end of the afternoon.

Perhaps you worked into the evening because there was so much to do, and by the time you left you were exhausted? If this happens to you on a regular basis, then it might be a clue that your relationship with work isn't quite as healthy as you think it is. Even if you're a high achiever – in fact, *especially* if you're a high achiever.

In the course of my work as a therapist, I often hear the phrase 'hard work: hard play' – usually when somebody is trying to justify the fact that they spend half their life getting drunk. You've probably heard phrases like this yourself, and know that they mean: 'I work hard, so now and then I like to let off some steam', or 'I work hard during the week so I like to party at weekends.' There's no harm in that, eh? Or is there?

Well, there's nothing wrong with having a strong work ethic – far from it – but the interaction between work and addiction is far more complex than you might imagine. You may be surprised to learn that work can become an addictive process in its own right, and it's capable of fuelling other addictions.

Working is a behaviour that can have a distinct mood-altering effect on us. It might not make us stagger around, in the way that being drunk does, but the impact it can have on our self-esteem is very profound.

Not everyone is affected by work in the same way, though. If someone goes out to do their job and comes home and gets on with their life in a normal way, they're unlikely to have a problem. Let's call that person Mr Average. He may or may not feel fulfilled by his job, but the point is, work isn't something that dominates every aspect of his life.

He eats well, he has healthy relationships outside of work, and he can function as a contented human being. If he achieves results in his job he feels good about it, but crucially, he isn't reliant on work as his only source of self-esteem.

When Work Stops Working

If you have an addictive nature, however, your relationship with work might end up being completely different. If you have a predisposition to anxiety (something from which I believe all addicts suffer), at some point in your life you're going to adapt your behaviour in an attempt to alleviate your discomfort. One way you might try to achieve this is by doing something that's mood altering – and work can seem like the ideal vehicle.

We sometimes hear people being labelled a workaholic as a backhanded compliment. But as a workaholic myself, I know it can cause very serious problems. In my case, I started work at a young age as a toolmaker in a factory, and I hated every minute of it. I couldn't stand the noise and the dirt, and in the mixed-up mind I had at the time, I wrongly thought my job was somehow demeaning. So, when the chance of a new career as a salesman came up, I jumped at it. Unfortunately, for someone who was utterly terrified of the world, as I was, there couldn't have been a worse job.

At first though, I loved it. I felt powerful and important as I headed off each morning in my slick suit, holding a briefcase. I travelled around the UK in a company car, selling designs for bar codes to the medical profession. What I didn't foresee was that the car and the suit came at a price: which was that I had to *perform*.

I soon realized that I only felt good when I made a decent sale. I'd spend the rest of the time in a state of high anxiety, worrying about how I was going to generate commission. All that stress only added to my growing booze problem. My work stopped working as a way of fixing me! I soon found myself getting up at dawn with a hangover and driving for hours to some faraway appointment at 9 a.m. I wanted to arrive early so I could get back up the motorway and into the pub again by lunchtime, when my working day ended.

To the outside world I looked like a successful young salesman, but inside I was thoroughly miserable. I was in a constant state of anxiety about whether or not I'd done enough to produce sufficient sales to keep my bosses happy, and for me to get a bonus. There was always a horrible trade-off between the work I put in and the anxiety it caused me, and in the end I didn't want to do *anything* because I felt so crap!

It was only many years later – after my life had eventually imploded due to booze – that I developed a healthier relationship with work. While I was in early recovery from alcoholism and drug abuse, I got my first job as a therapist, for which I was paid the equivalent of around £10,000 a year in today's money, which wasn't very much. The strange thing was, I'd never felt happier. I still worried about money, but I no longer needed a giant income to boost my ego, and therefore work caused me less anxiety.

I hear stories like my own all the time through my work as a therapist. Similar things occur right across the career spectrum. Very often, it's someone's relationship with work that's the high-octane fuel that drives other forms of addiction. They work too hard, so it drives them to drink – which in turn means they have to work even harder to make up for the time lost through boozing.

Generally, the more rewarding the job, the more potential there's to develop an unhealthy addiction to it. I believe this is one of the reasons we see such high incidences of alcoholism and drug abuse among professionals such as doctors, lawyers, bankers and journalists.

I have a friend who worked as a journalist on a national newspaper for many years. His life was one long, repetitive cycle of 12-hour working days, followed by 12-hour booze benders. As a result, he was constantly hungover at work, so he'd go to the gym to sweat it off. Then he'd have to work twice as hard to catch up with all the things he'd neglected while he'd had a hangover.

He loved the praise whenever he landed a big story, but most of his time was spent worrying about where the next scoop was coming from. He would have been far more productive if he'd just stuck to an eight-hour day and gone home and rested, but instead, he was always pushing himself too far. Unsurprisingly, he ended up in the Priory.

The Ticking Time Bomb

The process of gaining self-esteem through hard work usually starts at an early age, particularly among high achievers. Let's say, for example, that in childhood you do well in school. When you get good marks, it wins you praise and attention from your teachers or parents, which feels good. Nothing wrong with that – after all, it's natural for parents to want their children to do well at school. You enjoy the experience, so you work harder, and maybe, as a result, you do well in your final exams. The subsequent applause and affirmation feel even better. People start to praise you, and a place at university beckons. You think to yourself: *I like this. I feel clever and this is what I'm meant to do.*

Again, this is all fine and admirable. But if, deep down, you're suffering from emotional insecurity for whatever reason, then a subtle pattern could be beginning to emerge. You're starting to use work as a process to alleviate your distress – you're beginning to rely on it for your sense of self-worth.

Meanwhile, you go off to university and have a great time. Eventually, the process can bring great rewards, including qualifications, a good job and a high standard of living. But, due to your addictive nature, your relationship with work is like a ticking time bomb. You've come to rely on work so much – it's the most important thing in your life – that when you meet an unexpected obstacle in your career it can be devastating.

The point when it often becomes a major issue is when you hit a plateau in your career and realize for the first time that you might not go any higher up the ladder. You might have been driving onwards and upwards for years, but suddenly you find there's a ceiling. Maybe it's due to a boss who doesn't like you, or simply because the law of averages says that not everyone is going to make it to the very top.

That's when things start to unravel. It feels as if it's the end of your career, and you don't have a healthy and inherent sense of self-worth to see you through it. You might typically think: *I've got money in the bank but I'm working a 15-hour day and I feel like shit. I have no life or personal relationships outside work; what do I do now?*

I see lots of people between the ages of roughly 36 to 46 who've enjoyed meteoric rises within organizations, but hit a plateau when they suddenly realize they're not going to make it to CEO (or whatever position on the ladder they aspire to).

This could be through no fault of their own. For example, in any one hospital there are usually only one or two consultant cardiologists, but it doesn't mean the rest of the doctors are lacking in some way. But if someone has always relied on their career to make them feel good, suddenly there's an emotional void, and it causes a lot of anxiety.

> **As addicts, work has the potential to do three things that impact on us. It can give us affirmation; it can give us self-esteem; and it can provide the perfect distraction from problematic emotional issues that might otherwise be causing us distress.**

If you're looking for affirmation, a good job is the perfect opportunity because you're willing to work hard and you get excellent rewards for it. Going to university is just one of many routes that you might choose – there are plenty of other ways to channel your work ethic. So far, so good, because nobody has been hurt by this process to begin with.

But, as an addict, you aren't adept at doing certain things in moderation, especially anything that gives you a bit of a buzz: and self-esteem can be a very powerful buzz. So you begin to find that more and more of your life revolves around work. You're working 14 hours a day with no respite, and it's not much fun. You might be able to keep up the pace for many years, but negative consequences will eventually manifest themselves in lots of very subtle ways.

Maybe you'll go home exhausted every night and grab some junk food, or whatever is left over in the fridge, before crashing into bed. You'll get up the next morning and rush off to work again with the tank half empty. Perhaps your job will start to get in the way of other healthy things, like exercise and relationships, and you'll end up becoming depressed because you're not eating or relaxing properly.

You feel low, so you throw yourself into the one thing that gives you a lift: work. Pretty soon there's a negative dynamic going on in your life that acts as a vicious circle. You feel like shit because you're working too hard, so you work even harder to try and give yourself a lift. It might do the trick temporarily, but soon you're back where you started.

How is Your Relationship with Work?

Now, I don't want to suggest that everybody who works hard, or who enjoys their job, is a workaholic, but if the effect that work has on your life is increasingly negative, you may wish to ask yourself why that is.

Here are a few other questions that might give you some pointers as to whether you, or a loved one, may have a few issues around work:

⇨ Do you consider yourself to be a high achiever at work?

⇨ Do you regularly work though your lunch break?

⇨ Do you work extremely long hours? And does this impact on your home life?

⇨ Do you justify your overworking because you have an important job?

⇨ When you're not at work do you worry about work-related issues?

⇨ Do you find it difficult to have fun outside of work?

⇨ Do you find it hard to form relationships with people outside of work?

⇨ Do you find it hard to sleep well because you're stressed?

If you answer 'Yes' more times than 'No' to most of these questions, now ask yourself this: what is it that's stopping you from having a comfortable life? The answer could be that you are working *too* hard.

The signs that you might have a dysfunctional relationship with work can often be very subtle. For example, you might find it hard to go home at the end of a working day. I know one addict who always intended to leave his office at a reasonable hour, but when it came to it, he'd often lose himself in work and was still sat at his desk at 8 o'clock in the evening. It wreaked havoc with his marriage and his family felt neglected.

There can also be dire consequences for our health if we're locked in a pattern of poor eating habits and little relaxation because we're too busy working. Constant work itself can become stressful... and stress and anxiety are key triggers for addictive behaviour. The more we rely on our work as our only source of self-worth, the more likely it is that work itself becomes an addiction.

So, do you work in order to live, or do you live in order to work? If it's the latter, then you're at a much greater risk of having a problem on the horizon. The very thing that you've always relied on to improve the way you feel can itself become a source of constant anxiety. As we saw in earlier chapters, addicts are highly sensitive to praise or criticism from other people. This codependency on others for the way we feel can become a very dominant factor when it comes to our jobs. It feels great when we get a bonus, or some praise from the boss, but the boost is likely to be temporary.

The flipside is that we soon start to worry if we're not getting regular praise. If the boss hasn't said anything that's positive lately, we may start to worry that we're not doing quite as well as we could. We'll probably go out of our way to please our boss or our clients, which can become a bit of an obsession.

Maybe we start to work later and later because we're worried what our boss will think if he sees us going home bang on time. If we're anxious that the benefit we get from work is about to dry up, we have probably become a slave to our smartphone, always on the lookout for an email from the boss. It sounds pretty stressful, doesn't it? Sooner or later we might want to go and let off a bit of steam; after all, hard work leads to hard play...

When someone comes into rehab, it's normally because of an overt issue like booze, drugs or sex. That's the most obvious reason why they are there, so we tend to tackle that problem first. Therapists call this 'dealing with the alligator closest to the boat'. But sometimes work is the underlying problem that drives the overt problem.

There are many outlets for addictive behaviour, and they're not always obvious. The common factor is that the process is often fuelled by low confidence and low self-esteem, and sensitivity to emotional stress. To the outside world a person might seem affluent and successful, but inside they can be hurting like hell.

These negative feelings can trigger excessive drinking or drug taking – or they might manifest themselves in other ways. Some people start having affairs if they latch onto sex in an attempt to boost their self-esteem. They hate themselves for it, and they may have loving partners at home, but just like overworking, it becomes a compulsion that they cannot easily control.

Chapter 11

When Too Much Sex is Never Enough

People in the UK may remember the famous 'Hello Boys' advertising campaign for a certain lingerie manufacturer, back in 1994. When the giant billboards of an attractive model in her underwear were unveiled, they sparked a sensation and were blamed for stopping traffic and causing accidents as motorists and pedestrians stared up at them.

Today, sex is everywhere. If we open a newspaper or switch on the TV we're bombarded with sexual imagery, and there are countless magazines that devote page after page to it. The advertising industry is particularly adept at using sex to grab our attention. Sex has the power to captivate us, and it holds our focus like nothing else. It's also highly addictive.

If you were to ask the average person how they'd feel about the chance to have lots of sex on a daily basis, you'd probably get a fairly enthusiastic reaction, particularly from men. After all, sex is something that nature has programmed us to enjoy, and you'd be forgiven for thinking that it's the reason we're on the planet.

Our primary driving force, as a species, is to procreate, and judging from the population explosion over the last few generations, it's something that we're rather good at.

The obvious question that many people might ask, therefore, is whether sex addiction is a curse or a delight? Well, one thing that I'm certain of is that sex addiction is one of the most painful places a person can be.

Sex Affects Our Feelings

When I meet someone who has addictive issues connected to their sexual behaviour, I'm often struck by how dishevelled they look. I don't mean that their clothes are scruffy or dirty – I mean it's their faces that look drawn and distressed. They're clearly not having a good time, and their suffering is exacerbated by the enormous guilt and shame they feel – the taboos that surround sex are very powerful and they can have a very intense effect on our emotions.

Sex is very mood-altering – and like all things that can change the way we feel, it has the potential to become a compulsion that we find hard to control.

When we make love there are a number of physiological changes that take place in the brain that give us a strong buzz. There's a build up of adrenaline and excitement during the initial phase – it's a proactive high that makes us feel switched-on and alive.

This is followed by a release of endorphins in the brain during orgasm, the effect of which is to make us feel warm and contented. Nature has deliberately made sex a pleasurable experience so we want to keep coming back for more.

For the majority of the population this doesn't necessarily cause too many problems. Most people hopefully manage to strike a healthy balance between having sex and getting on with the rest of their lives. The thing that makes sex potentially problematic for those with an addictive nature, is that the buzz that it creates can be misused as a distraction from life's problems.

If we're feeling low or insecure, the temporary respite that sex provides can feel very seductive. The feelings of intense physical pleasure that it creates can seem like the perfect antidote for anxiety and low self-esteem. Afterwards we feel relieved and relaxed – at least that's the hope! Unfortunately, these benefits are usually very temporary, which means that if we have an addictive nature it can leave us constantly craving more.

Typically, men and women tend to draw their pleasure from sex in slightly different ways, although it's important to point out that this can differ from person to person. Many of the men I've counselled for sex addiction tend to focus very much on the physical act of sex itself. For them, sex is almost an automated response: something triggers them into becoming aroused and it sets them off down a path where they crave the physical pleasure that sex gives them.

For women, the benefit tends to be more about the emotional feelings of warmth and companionship that sex creates – and these feelings can be just as addictive.

How Sex Can Trigger Shame

It's precisely because sex has such a hold over us, that it can trigger intense feelings of guilt and shame. Much of this is due to cultural and religious influences that have evolved over thousands of years of human history.

The Bible teaches us that certain sexual scenarios are sinful, and this is something that's echoed across many religions. The story of Adam and Eve being corrupted in the Garden of Eden is a very powerful metaphor for the contradictory manner in which we regard sex. On the one hand we regard sex as something wonderful, and we celebrate the act of procreation, but on another level we think of it as sinful and naughty.

Because sex is so mood-altering it can cause us to do things that we might regret – like cheating on a partner or risking our sexual health. So, in order to live comfortably with sex, we need to learn to control our sexual urges in certain situations.

Our desire for sex needs to exist in parallel with the demands of normal living. This requirement to control our desires would have been particularly important for early humans. In primeval times, anyone who was distracted by sex at the wrong moment would have risked great danger. It would have been impossible to avoid predators if early humans were too busy procreating 24 hours a day! So they therefore evolved customs and taboos around sex – most obviously learning to cover their sexual organs in front of other people.

Religion took these customs to a whole new level of control. Many faiths celebrate celibacy as something pious and holy, whereas promiscuity is frowned upon. This has been the case throughout most of history. In Victorian times it was taken to new extremes, when those at the top of society were very puritanical about the manner in which they encouraged others to behave. This was very convenient if you happened to be a factory owner, because the last thing you wanted was your workforce constantly being distracted by sex.

If you can control the sexual habits of a population, you control the population. So, over the passage of time, sex became dirty and sinful. In many cultures, people are told that masturbation is bad for them. I can remember, as a young boy, being terrified by stories that it could cause hair to sprout on the perpetrator's palms and make them go blind.

But, despite everything, we still regard sex as deliciously naughty, which in turn becomes part of its allure. In this respect, it displays all the hallmarks of something that can become an addictive process. It's seductive and pleasurable, but the benefits are temporary. If you throw somebody with an addictive nature into the mix, then it's easy to understand how they can become hooked. This can manifest itself in lots of unexpected ways, such as constant masturbation or obsessive use of pornography, which, due to the internet, is more ubiquitous than ever before.

These types of activity can become a welcome distraction in times of stress, but they also trigger compulsive behaviour if we come to rely on them for their mood-altering effects. I've lost count of the number of rehab patients who tell me that they always masturbate before they go to sleep because it makes them feel relaxed. This might sound harmless, but it's unlikely to be the end of the story, because it's a step towards them using sex instead of their drug of choice.

What Is Sex Addiction?

Through my work, I've met people who are obsessed with sex. Their hunt for it becomes an all-consuming compulsion, but the moment they get it and achieve orgasm, the whole process starts again. Whatever it is they're seeking to fix through sex, they need to immediately fix it all over again.

This follows the same pattern that we take if we're addicted to booze, or binge on food. We feel like crap so we take a drink, or pig-out on doughnuts, to distract ourselves from our distress. But the relief is temporary and afterwards we feel even worse – so we repeat the behaviour.

Eventually, unwelcome consequences begin to set in – and these can be very extreme when it comes to the compulsive behaviours that surround sex. I know men who've given their partners sexually transmitted diseases, which they've caught while cheating on them. The guilt and shame this makes them feel is almost unimaginable, although when they're in the height of their addiction they're so ashamed that they'll deny they're responsible until they're blue in the face.

They'll use the addict's tools of minimization and will try to deceive their way out of their predicament. Deep down they're aware they're lying, and they can become very paranoid. Sometimes they may be convinced they've caught a sexually transmitted disease even if a casual encounter only took the form of fondling while high or drunk. Nonetheless, they insist on making a furtive trip to an STD clinic in order to get the all-clear – after which they revert to the same pattern of behaviour.

> **By the time a sex addict seeks help, their life can be in tatters. Very often they've encountered problems in the workplace as well as at home. This can be due to a lack of focus because they're always obsessing about sex, or it might be because they've made an unwanted pass at someone.**

Their behaviour becomes more and more extreme, and it might be that they encounter problems with the law – perhaps for exposing themselves in public or through downloading inappropriate material at work or in a domestic situation. People who are addicted to sex tend to look at lots of pornography, and after a while they may actually come to believe that some of the extreme things they see on a computer screen are normal. They may assume that people around them will want to behave in a similar fashion, but of course the reality is very different.

Sex addiction often exists in a cluster around other forms of addiction, particularly if someone is abusing alcohol and cocaine. Alcohol lowers our inhibitions, while cocaine stimulates our ego – which means when they're taken together they often lead to extreme forms of sexual behaviour.

I've known addicts who will drink copious amounts of alcohol before smoking crack cocaine with a prostitute, with whom they then have unprotected sex. They're playing Russian roulette with their own lives, and the lives of others, but they can't control their compulsion, no matter how shit it makes them feel.

Despite all the terrible things that may be going on in their life, problems with sex is usually the last thing a sex addict will admit to when they come into therapy – because it's the thing that causes them the most shame.

Often, a sex addict will begin by saying they're depressed. When I ask them why, they might volunteer that they're having difficulties at work or in holding down a relationship. But whatever they present as the problem, it's very rarely the real issue. It's only when I start talking in more depth that they might volunteer that they're also drinking heavily or using cocaine. Only then will it emerge that it's actually their sexual behaviour that's driving most of their distress.

This can lead sufferers into a very dark place – people who are sexually addicted can find themselves at risk from suicide, so I would strongly urge anyone who falls into this category to seek professional help.

The treatment sex addicts may need to undergo can be quite protracted, and it usually requires a long period of abstinence from all forms of sex, including masturbation. Often when I suggest this to somebody their face drops and they're incredulous, but it can be a very necessary part of their recovery.

Of course, there's nothing unhealthy about the act of masturbation – provided somebody is doing it because they feel genuinely aroused. If they are using masturbation as a way of medicating their feelings, the classic circle of diminishing returns will set in, and their behaviour will become more and more extreme as they seek out new highs.

In severe situations this can cause a large amount of shame and distress. I've heard of cases in which female sex addicts have spent a whole night having sex with multiple partners. This behaviour makes the women feel terrible afterwards, and the effect it has on their self-esteem is soul-destroying.

Men who've had a large number of sexual partners tend to brush it off with bravado, but women fear being branded a slag or a trollop in the eyes of society, which only serves to exacerbate their distress. The truth is that sex addiction is damaging, regardless of gender or sexual orientation.

Treating Sex Addiction

When a person goes into treatment for sex addiction we sometimes recommend that they adhere to a *'Three Second Rule'*. This is a form of treatment whereby if they spot someone to whom they're attracted – for example, a good-looking stranger on the train – they must look away within three seconds as a way of preventing them from obsessing about sex with that person.

Sometimes the therapy that's recommended also includes operating the *'Three Circle System'*. This is where a range of behaviours are listed as being within the bands of three concentric circles. The inner circle contains things that are forbidden, such as downloading pornography or visiting a prostitute. The middle band contains risky behaviour that's best avoided. This might include picking up a magazine that's likely to contain sexual images. The outer circle contains things that are acceptable – which would include going to dinner with someone with whom you have a healthy relationship.

This may sound like a lot of rules and regulations around sex, but in the case of an addict it's often the best course of action in order to recalibrate their lifestyle. For example, some men will need to relearn how to visit a shopping centre without automatically attempting to look up women's skirts as they travel on the escalator.

Others may crave sex in public places. This occurs particularly in gay men who may have previously sought out partners in public toilets. The risk of being caught may have added to their thrill, and this in turn may have further fuelled their addiction. Avoiding the sort of places where they may have had sex in the past is important.

Of course, not every addict has issues around sex – and nor are all people who enjoy an active sex life addicted. So how can you tell if you're likely to develop certain issues or problems around sex? Well, just like other forms of addiction, a lot depends on the effect that the process has on your feelings. There's nothing shameful or dirty about having a lot of healthy sex – and that includes heterosexual or homosexual sex, or masturbation.

However, what does matter is the *reason* you crave sex, and the *consequences* of it. If you find yourself masturbating in private because you're feeling horny, that's a normal thing to do. But if you're doing it because, deep down, you're sick with worry or feeling stressed, then that's not so healthy.

If you're doing it because you're trying to heal yourself, it won't work – and sooner or later negative consequences will set in. Similarly, if you're in a relationship and you find yourself feeling shit because you're constantly cheating on your partner, then it may be time to ask yourself why you're doing it.

Alternatively, if you're single, it might be that you're using sex as a way of boosting your emotional self-esteem. This is a behaviour that I've seen many times in women who feel vulnerable and insecure. If they're codependent on others to heal their feelings, sex can become their means of seeking affirmation. It might not necessarily mean that they sleep around with multiple partners – but if they crave the thrill of a new relationship, this can develop into what amounts to an addiction to love.

When the initial rush of a new relationship passes, the benefits soon wear off and they may move on to the next relationship, normally encountering a lot of pain and anxiety along the way. Fortunately, there are a number of very good self-help groups that can provide assistance, many of them for free. You can find examples of these in Appendix 2 of this book.

In the meantime, if hot and cold running sex sounds appealing, be careful what you wish for. Sometimes too much sex is never enough.

Chapter 12

Drugs: The Many Roads to Hell

When we talk about addiction to drugs we typically think of heroin. It's a drug that's portrayed as the demon lurking on every street corner, ready to spread its filthy tentacles around anybody foolish enough to succumb to its lure. In the eyes of the media, heroin has become the epitome of evil: corrupting anyone who goes near it.

We're all familiar with the image of a junkie shooting up in a filthy squat before passing into a stupor, like something from a scene in Danny Boyle's drugs movie *Trainspotting*. So it might surprise you to learn that heroin began life as a substance that was not only perfectly legal, but also routinely prescribed by doctors for common ailments such as coughs, colds and diarrhoea.

The word 'Heroin' is a brand name invented by the German pharmaceutical company Bayer for one of two legal wonder drugs that it developed at the end of the 19th century. The other drug was Aspirin, so Bayer had simultaneously created the world's best drug and what was to become regarded as the world's worst drug.

Initially, it was heroin that looked like being the best banker. As a painkiller it was eight times stronger than morphine, and when prescribed in moderation it seemed like the ideal pick-me-up for a range of minor ailments. In 1956, the drug was outlawed in the UK, prompting an outraged leader column in *The Times* newspaper entitled 'The Case for Heroin'.

Such a headline would be unthinkable today, but *The Times* may have actually got it right, all those years ago, because one thing that I'm now absolutely certain of is that our modern social policy towards heroin and other Class A drugs is deeply flawed.

Our Drugs Policy Isn't Working

In 1956, there were just 317 registered addicts of 'manufactured drugs' in Great Britain, of whom 47 were addicted to heroin. If you go onto the National Treatment Agency/NHS websites today, you'll see that, according to the latest figures, there are now 298,752 'opiate/crack users' in the UK.[8]

In the 50 years since we decided to tackle drug addiction via the criminal justice system, the problem has increased in size almost *1,000 times!* Clearly, something isn't working.

The fact that heroin was once regarded as a safe drug, and it was handed out by GPs, illustrates just how polarized our attitude to drugs has become. We see everything in terms of good or bad. Legal drugs are regarded as good, and illegal drugs are regarded as bad. But if heroin was once legal – and widely prescribed – then surely we can't have it both ways?

In my opinion, what this actually shows is that it doesn't matter whether the substance you're addicted to is legal or not, the consequences can be just as harmful. Indeed, the manner in which a substance is classified often appears to be purely arbitrary.

When it comes to addiction, it's not the nature of a substance that's wholly to blame: it's also down to the habits of users and the reasons why they take it. The drugs themselves obviously have addictive properties, but they don't necessarily cause addiction on an emotional level unless other factors come into play. I'm not for one minute trying to argue that heroin is a harmless substance. Far from it. I'm the first to acknowledge that it causes a great deal of suffering, and I've seen first-hand the misery and despair endured by heroin addicts, many of whom are doomed to die a horrific death as a result of their habit. I wouldn't recommend its recreational use to anybody. However, what I am saying is that criminalizing it is not the answer.

I'm convinced that being addicted to legal substances, such as alcohol and nicotine, or prescription drugs, can be just as serious, and in some cases more dangerous, than heroin.

In almost every modern country booze and cigarettes kill far more people than heroin does. In many Western societies the biggest killer of all is actually obesity, due to over-consumption of sugary food. Yet we don't even widely regard sugar as being addictive.

What matters for understanding addiction isn't so much the legal status of a drug, it's the effect it has upon us, and the reasons that we abuse it. Clearly, not everybody who drinks alcohol is an alcoholic, and it would be preposterous to even suggest that.

Similarly, not everybody who takes drugs on a recreational basis is an addict (although granted, the majority probably are). Some will dabble only occasionally, while others may use certain drugs on a semi-regular basis, but they'll have no major problems quitting when the circumstances of their lifestyle require them to do so.

For example, during the Vietnam War, large numbers of American GIs regularly used heroin while they were in Southeast Asia. When they returned to the USA, the vast majority of them stopped. Only around 10 per cent – roughly the same proportion of the population that I estimate suffer from an addictive nature today – continued to take it.

So what is it that defines addictive consumption of a substance, as opposed to recreational or social use? Well, here's one possible way of discovering a clue.

A good way to find out if you're using a substance in an addictive manner is to ask yourself a very simple question: does it cost you more than you pay for it?

This simple acid test can be applied to everything from alcohol consumption right through to regular abuse of an illegal substance such as cocaine. For example, if you drink regularly but it doesn't cause you any negative consequences, I'll be the first to wish you all the best. But if the true cost of your drinking includes damage to your health, or to your relationships or to your self-esteem (or anything else), you need to evaluate what the overall cost is (as clearly, it's a lot more than just the price of the booze).

If so, is it a price you're willing to pay? Are the consequences of your drinking becoming increasingly negative as time goes on? You can use the same approach to assess drug use. The answers to these questions are always likely to be dictated by the reasons why you take a substance – and it's usually one of two effects that you're looking for.

'Uppers' and 'Downers'

In most cases of drug abuse, the user tends to be seeking out one or the other of two different effects: these are either 'nurturant' or 'hedonistic'. With *nurturant* drug abuse, the user is seeking to medicate themselves in order to chill out and relax. If you have an addictive nature, this is the perfect way to forget about all that background anxiety and emotional pain that you experience due to your overactive limbic system. Alternatively, with *hedonistic* drug abuse, the user is seeking to get high and wants to feel great. If you have an addictive nature, hedonistic use can also be a way of overcoming emotional pain and sensitivity.

In both cases, the process may be subconscious rather than conscious. You don't necessarily think to yourself that you can't 'take' life today – you just go out and get smashed. These two different types of drug use might also be described as taking 'uppers' or 'downers'. Some substances can have both effects, depending on the context in which they are taken, and the amount that's consumed by the user.

Nurturant Drugs

These are the 'downers', like **heroin** and other opiates, some of which are legal – such as **codeine**. They have a strong propensity to create physical dependency, and in this sense they're highly addictive. Very few heroin users begin by injecting the drug – in fact, I've never come across anybody who started out by using the drug intravenously.

What tends to happen is that people start off by being introduced to smoking it by a friend. Because it's such a strong downer, it doesn't give you a feeling of euphoria as such, just an intense sense of inner peace. Given the horrific consequences that can follow, these feelings of peace are dangerously deceptive, but nonetheless they're very seductive. Heroin typically comes in the form of a brown powder, which is burned on foil and the fumes are inhaled to give the desired effect.

> **The problem with all nurturant drugs is that, sooner or later, you have to return to reality if your life is to function in any meaningful way.**

That's when the problems set in, because if you've been taking the drug to medicate away distress or anxiety, you can bet your life that these feelings are going to be all the more acute when the effects of the drug wear off.

Often, the feelings are much *worse* than they were before, which in turn triggers an urge for even more of the drug. As the addictive cycle progresses, many heroin users switch to injecting (mainlining) the drug into their veins. This is incredibly dangerous because street heroin is often cut with all sorts of horrible substances and poisons in order to make it go further.

There are also hygiene issues; there can be dire consequences if needles are not sterile. Many heroin abusers develop horrific ulcers all over their body as they search out new places to inject the drug. Eventually, their veins start to collapse and they may resort to injecting into painful places like their groin in their desperation to chase a hit.

There's a strong risk of fatal overdose, which is often due to the rogue ingredients that the heroin is cut with. And just to complicate the picture, the user may typically take other drugs like cocaine and alcohol at the same time as they're on heroin.

In my opinion, the explosion in heroin abuse is partly due to the fact that it has been heavily criminalized. There's a famous scene in *Trainspotting* in which Ewan McGregor's character declares: 'We would have injected vitamin C if only they had made it illegal.'

Ironically, I think there's a lot of truth to this. By demonizing heroin, the authorities have helped to create a whole subculture that now surrounds its supply and usage. Just as outlawing booze during Prohibition backfired in the USA in the 1920s, banning heroin has led to an explosion of organized crime. I've no doubt that heroin is a dangerous substance that needs controlling, but I can't see the point of fully criminalizing its use because that approach simply isn't working. Instead, we should concentrate on tackling the true causes of addiction – which exist within the human condition of the addicts themselves.

Unfortunately, we fail to do this in the UK, and concentrate instead on dishing out a heroin substitute called **methadone** to registered addicts. I cannot think of a worse approach – in my view this is simply crazy because all it's doing is perpetuating the problem by switching one dangerous drug for another.

The reason doctors do it is because methadone is legal under prescription, whereas heroin is illegal. Methadone does not give a user the same intense nurturant effect as heroin, so their thinking is that it's easier to wean addicts off it than heroin. But unfortunately that doesn't happen – and methadone users continue to be trapped in the same cycle of misery.

Methadone is typically prescribed as a green liquid that addicts are asked to drink in view of a pharmacist – but many addicts manage to smuggle it away and sell it in order to buy heroin. In some respects methadone is a more dangerous drug than heroin, because it has a lower tolerance range. Users only need to overdose by a relatively small percentage in order to suffer serious medical problems, or even death.

> **Many heroin addicts simply use methadone as a supplement to their wider drug use – it gets them through the day while they attempt to score enough cash to buy more drugs in the evening.**

In addition to heroin, other drugs that fall into the category of downers, or nurturant drugs, include prescription **tranquilizers** that belong to the **benzodiazepine** family. The chief purpose of these drugs is to tackle anxiety, but they're highly addictive.

This is an area in which I speak from bitter experience, because for 30 years I was addicted to a benzodiazepine called Lorazepam. I went to my doctor and explained that I was having problems coping with life because I was constantly plagued by feelings of anxiety and fear. Lorazepam is a drug that takes away anxiety and leaves you feeling nothing in the world is a problem. It's a bit like an anaesthetic for emotional pain in that respect.

My problem was that, at the time, I was also drinking vast amounts of Jack Daniels on top if it. I was hopelessly addicted, and whenever I tried to stop taking Lorazepam, the anxiety would return with a fierce vengeance.

Some nurturant drugs, like codeine for example, are available over the counter without a prescription. There are numerous cases I've come across of people being addicted to **Nurofen Plus** (which contains codeine) because it gives them a feeling of tranquillity. Codeine is a powerful drug in its own right – and many heroin users will seek it out to take the edge off their distress if they cannot get hold of heroin itself. Unfortunately, in high doses, Nurofen Plus also causes extreme medical complications, not least because it also contains Ibuprofen, which can cause stomach problems when taken in excess.

Cannabis is also a nurturant drug that many people smoke for its relaxing properties. It can cause numerous health problems, including severe paranoia. It also acts as a stepping stone to harder drugs (which I'll talk about later).

Finally, as I said earlier, some substances cross the divide and can act both as uppers *and* downers. This is true of **alcohol** and **nicotine**, both of which can act either as a stimulant or a relaxant, depending on the amount consumed and the mood of the user.

Hedonistic Drugs

The typical drug of choice for hedonistic users is **cocaine**, which is also highly addictive. It's a stimulant that makes the user feel invincible, boosting their confidence and making them feel as if there's not a challenge in the world they cannot meet. Users experience a huge rush of euphoria when they take it for the first time, but they're unlikely to ever achieve quite the same buzz again, at least not without continually increasing the dosage that they take.

Heavy use can lead to heart problems and severe paranoia and psychosis. People who use cocaine can very often still function and hold down good jobs (which they need in order to be able to afford their habit). But as they use more and more cocaine their ability to function gets less and less.

They'll normally also be heavy drinkers, and can act out their addiction through sexual behaviour, for example by sleeping with prostitutes. If somebody has been using cocaine for a long time it can give them heart palpitations, which make them feel awful. If their drinking is also out of control, they'll often end up in a treatment centre. Cocaine and alcohol, when combined, create a third substance in the liver called cocaethylene, which can cause heart attacks.

> **The effect that addicts are looking for, regardless of whether they take nurturant or hedonistic substances, is to change the way that they feel. That's why it doesn't really matter what the legal status of the substance is.**

One substance on the hedonistic side that many people consider to be the worst in its effects is a derivative of cocaine called **crack cocaine**. This consists of powdered cocaine that has been washed of its impurities by chemicals in order to turn it into little rocks, which are then smoked. It gives a very, very intense high, which is then followed by a very, very intense low. Typically, crack cocaine addicts can use for days on end, until they run out of money or they're exhausted.

In my opinion, the most dangerous of the hedonistic drugs is **crystal meth** – which gives users a huge high that lasts for a long time. The come down is so bad that people literally can't stand it. They can't cope with the physical and psychological withdrawal, so there have been instances of addicts going out and committing murder to get money to pay for their next high. In the UK, it's linked to use within the gay community, because it lowers sexual inhibitions. My advice to anyone is to avoid crystal meth at all costs.

Ecstasy is another hedonistic drug, although very different to crystal meth in its effects. It creates feelings of intense euphoria and happiness, but like all addictive substances, there's a price to pay later on if you become hooked on it. Some people may also derive a nurturant effect from ecstasy, so, like booze and cigarettes, it has a foot in both camps as an upper and a downer.

Clearly, abuse of illegal drugs involves some form of interaction with the criminal underworld, which brings its own risks and complications. However, what worries me far more than this is the fact that the medical profession is one of the biggest pushers of all. By dishing out tranquilizers, anti-depressants and substitute drugs like methadone, the UK's National Health Service is institutionally biased towards tackling the *symptoms* of addiction, rather than the psychological and emotional factors that *cause* the condition. Meanwhile by criminalizing, rather than controlling, certain substances, we're throwing petrol onto the flames.

If you calculate the entire number of deaths caused annually in the UK by illegal drugs it comes to just a few thousand. In 2008, the United Nations Office on Drugs and Crime (UNODC) estimated the figure to be 2,278.[9] But if you were to combine the true death toll caused by booze, smoking and obesity, in my opinion it would be likely to run to many hundreds of thousands.

Unfortunately, there are no reliable figures, as many obesity or alcohol-related deaths are the underlying causes of other illnesses (and are therefore reported as something else). The UK's National Office for Statistics estimates that in 2011 there were 8,748 deaths directly connected to alcohol,[10] but the true figure will be many times higher.

What we do know for sure is that lung cancer – caused in the main by nicotine addiction – is a major cause of death in adult males.

According to the campaign group ASH, smoking kills around 100,000 people in the UK every year.[11] That's almost 300 people a day! Imagine the outcry if there was a similar death toll on the roads, or in the aviation industry. If a plane crashed near Heathrow every day, killing hundreds of people, we would do something about it very quickly.

Banning drugs and criminalizing their usage isn't the answer – what we need to do is start by acknowledging that addiction is a psychological and emotional problem, rather than a physical dependency issue.

I've one final thought, with which I'll close this chapter: if the figures for nicotine deaths are shocking, I'm afraid they're nothing compared to the growing death toll from obesity. Food addiction is something that takes society's problems to a whole new level. There's a lack of detailed data for the combined death toll from illnesses caused by obesity in the UK, which is part of the problem. However, studies in the USA suggest that it could account for 18 per cent in that country – that's nearly one in five deaths.

Chapter 13

Do You Overdose on Anger?

Many years ago, when I was a heavy drinker, a member of my family bought me a little plaque with a sign on it to hang on the wall. The sign stated that there are two sides to every argument: 'Mine and the wrong one'. The message to me was clear: I always had to be seen to be in the right, no matter what.

It was an amusing catchphrase, but it actually contained a very important clue about what it's like to live with someone who has an addictive nature. Most alcoholics and addicts *hate* to lose an argument, and they absolutely *detest* it if people perceive them to be in the wrong about something. It makes them grumpy, riled or very, very angry.

In my house, whenever a politician opened his or her mouth to speak in a TV studio debate, my family would run for cover. They knew that, sooner or later, I'd be ranting and raving about the state of the world, because I disagreed with almost everything that I heard on TV. It was very simple: I was in the right and the rest of the world was wrong.

Thankfully, now that I'm a bit older and hopefully a tiny bit wiser, I know that the reason I was like this was because, deep down, I was insecure. I just didn't feel good enough about life in general, but I was too weak to accept that I could ever be in the wrong.

I had no inner confidence to tackle the emotional ups and downs that life threw at me, and so the only way I could rectify this was to convince myself I was always in the right. It didn't matter whether it was a dispute in a relationship or an argument about something as trivial as the price of fish: I *always* knew best (or so I thought).

I see this sort of character trait in others all the time in my work as an addiction therapist.

> **Often when I talk to somebody who's in treatment they'll acknowledge that their life is in a mess, but they still think they're right about almost everything they do. They simply can't bear the idea of being wrong.**

In a situation like that, I sometimes go to a whiteboard and draw a gravestone. I put 'RIP' on it, above the person's name, with an epitaph that says: 'This person was always right!' I do this to demonstrate how preposterous the idea is that anyone can always be perfect... but it doesn't stop addicts getting very angry whenever they're challenged.

The Root of Anger Is Fear

Most addictive processes are driven by an inability to deal with our feelings – and one of the most powerful emotions that we can experience is anger. It can be overwhelming in its intensity. Anger can make us rant and rave; it can make us behave in ways towards other people that are simply insane, and it can end in outbursts of uncontrolled violence.

But what exactly *is* anger, and why does it exist as an emotion? Well, if you look at it from a physiological perspective, anger is a defence mechanism that's triggered by *fear*.

If something makes you angry, it's nearly always because it has the potential to make you feel afraid, or at the very least, very insecure. It might not always be immediately obvious, but anger is a coping mechanism for dealing with fear.

Here's an example that proves this point. Let's say you're out in your car when another motorist cuts in front of you. You react angrily and before you know it you're involved in a road rage incident. What actually happens is that, deep down, your behaviour is triggered by fear. Of course, you don't consciously think of it like that. The red mist simply descends and you go into a rant. But on an emotional level your limbic system has kicked in because you perceived a threat to your wellbeing, and this triggers fear.

It may be that you were afraid that the other road user's driving could have harmed you. Or maybe the fear was just triggered by the disrespect the other person showed you (after all, if they get away with treating you like shit then others will too). Either way, it unleashes your anger. Often there's a clue to what's going on in the language that you choose to express your anger:

'What the fuck do you think you're doing? You could have killed me...' or *'Who the hell do you think you are, treating me like that?'*

What you're really saying is: *'I was afraid I was going to get hurt'*, or *'I'm fearful that by treating me like that, you think that you're better than me.'*

As we saw earlier, our limbic system reacts to threats through fight, flight or freeze. If you're going to fight, you need to be fired up, with adrenaline pumping and your senses heightened. A very effective mechanism to achieve this state is anger. But it doesn't matter whether the anger you feel is righteous or imagined – it's still driven by fear.

When I was ranting and raving at the TV, it was because I was secretly afraid that the rest of the world was better than me, so

I reacted in the only way I knew how to at the time, which was through anger. But my anger wasn't the enemy: it was fear. If you have an addictive personality then fear is likely to be your constant companion... and fear is the No. 1 driver of anger.

> **Fear can be triggered by lots of different things, but at its heart is usually a deep-rooted insecurity about one's own self-worth. If you're frightened about life in general, anger works so well as a coping mechanism that you can actually experience the equivalent of a high from it.**

When you're full of fury you don't feel frightened and you don't care about your insecurities – all you care about is expressing your rage. The feelings of strength and invincibility that anger can create within us are a welcome release from all the insecurity and anxiety. Suddenly, you feel powerful, whereas normally there's only fear.

In some scenarios, anger can become a permanent part of your nature, so that you become irritable and borderline aggressive all of the time. We've probably all had colleagues like this in the workplace. People tend to walk on eggshells whenever they're around this person, because they seem to be spoiling for an argument the whole time.

If you add alcohol to a mix like that it can be like tossing a match into a box of fireworks. If somebody has anger issues then the booze is likely to aggravate things. I've been in plenty of bars and stood drinking with guys who are constantly on the lookout for any slight, either real or perceived, which they can use as an excuse to explode. They might be big burly men who give the impression of relishing violence, but in my experience their actions are always driven by insecurity.

I can recall being in pubs in my hometown where anybody overheard speaking in a middle-class accent risked being punched. The reason for this would invariably be that the attacker was reacting to feelings of being 'Less Than' – in other words, they were afraid of being perceived as inferior to someone.

Often it's the people with the most aggression who carry the most fear – and woe betide anyone who gets in their way. The anger becomes a compulsive behaviour in its own right – one that forms a very active part of the addictive process.

Anger is usually the result of experiences in childhood, and someone may have been carrying it around for many years. If, for example, somebody spent most of their childhood being picked on by their siblings, or in the presence of a violent parent, then they're likely to have developed an angry fight response just to exist. The resentments and negative feelings will have become part of their core being.

> **The result is that they're always on the lookout for slights, or excuses to react with aggression and anger. Alcohol can quickly unleash these resentments, which in extreme cases results in an urge to batter the hell out of anyone who comes within range.**

I've counselled many individuals for anger management and when you look underneath their anger you'll always find fear. They suffer from a form of codependency whereby their own feelings of self-worth are dictated by the actions of others. They have low self-worth – and they cannot stand the idea of anybody thinking ill of them.

The only way they can feel better and gain self-esteem is through the affirmation of others. But if anybody acts towards them in a way that they perceive as disrespectful, that's when the fireworks start. None of this is necessarily a conscious process: they just go through life with a temper that's resting on a hair-trigger.

Compulsive Helpers

The fear and anxiety that people with an addictive nature feel so acutely can sometimes have a very interesting flipside. Instead of reacting with anger towards others, it can make us overbearing in our need to *help* others. The goal is still the same: to increase our own self-worth by gaining approval from other people.

If you have a low opinion of yourself because your childhood experiences left you convinced that you're a piece of shit, then it's only through affirmation from other people that you can change this. The result can be a behaviour known as *compulsive helping,* which I alluded to in earlier chapters.

This occurs when you become super-attuned to the needs of others as a way of fixing yourself. The only way you feel okay is if they're okay – so you end up getting your buzz by putting right the problems of everybody around you, while ignoring your own needs. Compulsive helping occurs when you carry out actions to help or control the lives of other people to the point where it becomes an obsession and results in harm to either yourself or them.

There are two types of compulsive helpers: dominant and submissive. The dominant ones tend to be very controlling of others, and this typically manifests itself in the workplace. They're the people who, like me, truly believe that their side of an argument is *always* the right one. In this respect, they come across as a bit of a control freak.

A friend of mine is a recovering addict who once worked in the technology industry. He'd typically chair meetings where there were 15 or 20 people working together on a project, but, instead of delegating, he would insist that everything was done his way, right down to the last minor detail. Not only did he nearly work himself to death, but he also irritated almost everybody around him, because nobody was allowed to do their own job without his interference.

I've come across lots of people like this who work in high-pressure industries such as banking or the media. They need to be in charge of others in order to feel okay about themselves. What they're actually seeking is affirmation and approval from their peers. These positive reactions from others give them a buzz, and it helps alleviate their own inner feelings of fear and anxiety.

A dominant compulsive helper always wants to get *everybody* to do things their way, so unsurprisingly it often ends in confrontation – which only adds to their problems. They risk becoming burned out as they take the responsibilities of others onto their own shoulders. They can be very cunning and manipulative, but unfortunately it results in a meltdown because they take on too much. Their actions also make them highly unpopular, which aggravates their secret feelings of low self-worth and fear.

Submissive compulsive helpers behave in a slightly different way, but just like their dominant counterparts they start out by seeking approval and affirmation. Their actions towards other people, such as family members, friends, neighbours and workmates, can be very caring and helpful. They'll often be the first to offer help to a friend in need and can show great kindness.

For example, they might offer to do the shopping, help with the cleaning and run errands. The approval and thanks they receive in return make them feel good about themselves. Of course, there's nothing wrong with being thoughtful of others – but in compulsive helpers it runs completely out of control. They end up doomed to a life of running round after everyone else, to the point where their own needs and the needs of their loved ones may be neglected.

> I've encountered people who spend their whole life shopping or running errands for others – and they love nothing more than listening while a friend pours out all their troubles to them. They end up with the weight of the world on their shoulders, unable to function on an emotional level in their own right.

Unfortunately, even the people they're seeking to help may end up being harmed if they come to rely too heavily on the compulsive helper. They can no longer fight their own battles because someone has always done it for them.

Compulsive helping may start out with positive intentions, but the helper ends up becoming a hopeless 'do-gooder' who can no longer see the wood for the trees while their own life collapses and resentments start to build up.

It may well be that some people can display both forms of compulsive helping, dominant and submissive, depending on the circumstances they find themselves in. Someone who works in a bank or in the media may be very submissive towards their own boss, but then be a completely controlling ogre towards the people below them. A compulsive helper may also lean towards a role in a Human Resources team, or take a highly paid career as a personal assistant. If you love organizing the lives of others, then where better to work than HR? Similarly, if you want to run around after someone important, becoming a PA may appeal.

In my own case, while I was quite happy to be dominant of others, I was not beyond also dabbling in submissive compulsive helping. I'd start off by offering to help somebody but it soon became a chore that I resented. I remember on one occasion offering to drive a neighbour to the airport. I refused to accept any money from them for petrol: I was doing them a favour (wasn't I great!)

At first they made a big fuss about what a nice person I was, and I felt good about it. But the next time they asked they weren't quite so flattering, and there was no offer to contribute towards the petrol. On the *third* occasion I did it, I was beginning to feel like an unpaid taxi driver and I drove to the airport simmering with resentment.

I vowed to tell my neighbour to go and fuck himself if he ever had the cheek to ask me again. My actions were typical compulsive helping, because they involved an imaginary profit and loss account. I was happy to help – but I wanted my pound of flesh in return, in the form of adulation and affirmation.

Of course, getting angry from time to time doesn't mean you're an addict. Neither does being helpful towards others. But if either becomes a coping mechanism for fear, you might find it's time to ask yourself what it is that's *causing* that fear...

Chapter 14

Anorexia, Bulimia, Overeating and Self-Harming

If you go onto YouTube and type in the word 'anorexia' something very disturbing happens. You'll see video after video containing harrowing photographs of skeletal young women. Many of the girls are so emaciated that their bodies are clearly in danger of shutting down through lack of nourishment.

The pictures are so shocking that you need to do a double take. They're hauntingly reminiscent of images of concentration camp victims.

The women's ribs protrude from their saggy skin and the bumps of their spines are clearly visible down the length of their backs. Some of the videos are posted as warnings about the dangers of eating disorders, but it's my belief that many of them have a much darker purpose. The pictures on display are often self-portraits taken by anorexia sufferers who are posing in front of mirrors.

The garish photos fade from one to another while trendy pop music plays in the background. The message is clear: 'Look at me; don't I look great?' Not only are the anorexics willing to display their bodies, but they are also proud of the way they look – horrific as that may seem.

Anorexics suffer from a condition called body dysmorphia. In this, the sufferer becomes obsessively worried about some aspect of his or her appearance, such as their weight. It leads to them having a distorted view of their own body shape.

When they look at themselves in the mirror anorexics don't see someone who is close to starvation; instead, in their own mind, they see someone who needs to slim, and they aspire to lose even more weight. It illustrates the power that eating disorders can have over people – and it makes their condition very hard to treat.

People with an addictive nature often use their relationship with food as a way of medicating their negative feelings and their emotional problems. The eating disorders they develop tend to fall into three distinct categories. These are anorexia, bulimia and overeating (which I touched on in the earlier chapter about sugar).

Anorexia manifests itself through starvation due to the avoidance of food. Sufferers become painfully thin and they may go for many days on end without eating a single thing. Bulimia, meanwhile, is when somebody binges on food, but they maintain a normal weight by purging their body by inducing themselves to vomit. In contrast, people who *over*eat gorge daily, over a long period of time, and their weight balloons to gargantuan proportions.

A strange aspect of these three distinct types of eating disorder is that a sufferer may potentially swap from one state to another as time goes on. For example, if somebody is anorexic they may swap to bingeing on food and force themselves to throw up (in which case they develop bulimia), or they may even go on to become an overeater.

All three types of eating disorder are self-harming in their nature.

Anorexia

Many people don't readily see anorexia as a form of addiction, but that's exactly what it is. The sufferer becomes addicted to the effect that the anorexia has on their feelings – and in particular on the control that they perceive it gives them over their body.

Avoiding food becomes a compulsion that's rooted in the same causes that drive other types of addictive behaviour. These are usually fear, insecurity, low self-confidence and an inability to deal with emotional pain. At the heart of anorexia – as with all addictive processes – lies codependency. It's an emotional and psychological condition.

> **If someone's life feels out of control, being very rigid about what they eat may feel like a way of reasserting some order. It's the reason why an anorexic is very iron-willed about how to control what they eat. The need to avoid food becomes a compulsive obsession.**

The feelings generated by the process of starvation become a distraction from the emotional distress that the sufferer would otherwise be feeling due to other factors in their life or childhood.

Of course, far from giving them control, what actually happens is that the eating disorder comes to control *them*. It may spill over into other areas of their life aside from food.

Anorexia is about avoidance: and this can manifest itself into avoiding sex, avoiding intimacy, and even the avoidance of spending money. Typically, an anorexic will be very scared of sex, and they'll go to great lengths to avoid the intimacy it involves. Others will make a huge effort to avoid spending cash, forcing themselves to live a very austere existence, or to rely on others for their financial needs.

It's important to note that anorexia does not just affect women. We're starting to see an increasing number of boys in treatment centres who are anorexic. In fact, I suspect it's a condition that has affected males throughout history, but it may have been misdiagnosed as other illnesses in the past.

Anorexia is a mechanism for control, and this manifests itself in all sorts of ways. Strange as it may seem, a tell-tale sign of whether or not someone has an eating disorder can often be found in the shape of their handwriting. Anorexics tend to have the smallest, neatest handwriting in the world.

They'll write line after line of little tidy script, all perfectly formed. Bulimics and overeaters tend to write in slightly bigger letters, but they're still very perfect in their formation. This too often gives me a clue that someone is trying to exert a lot of control over their handwriting, just as they do with their diet.

Anorexics exhibit willpower that can be extraordinarily strong. As a way of breaking the ice with them I often joke that I'd want them on my side in a war because they're so strong-willed! They're highly astute and intelligent, and more than capable of working out that their life isn't as they would like it to be.

Unfortunately, the path they choose in order to try and fix things is highly destructive and it follows the classic addictive process. They feel like shit, so they starve themselves. The physiological effect that this creates gives them a temporary reassurance that they're dealing with their problems. They get high on being light-headed from starvation.

Of course, sooner or later, they need to eat *something* to survive, which makes them feel guilty and disgusted with themselves. They feel like shit again, which triggers a repeat of the whole process. Body dysmorphia exacerbates this process because they may be convinced that they're as fat as an elephant, whereas in reality they're actually unnaturally skinny.

Occasionally an anorexic may allow themselves to indulge in a 'forbidden' food like ice cream. This can trigger temporary feelings of euphoria, which are quickly followed by more shame and disgust for losing control. Anorexics are also prone to over-exercising in an attempt to burn off calories. I've known girls who will go out of their way to walk many miles every day as they try to lose weight. They may also resort to swallowing laxatives in large doses to further accentuate their weight loss.

The internet may play a large role in an anorexic's behaviour, as they typically exchange tips and advice on so-called 'pro-ana' bulletin boards (which also contain the sort of videos that appear on YouTube). Some of this advice is very detailed and it can make harrowing reading. I know of one case in which a teenage girl was advised to sleep with her bedroom window wide open so that her body would burn more calories in the cold.

The mainstream media is often accused of triggering anorexic behaviour by presenting skinny fashion models as icons for girls to aspire to. I believe there's some truth in this, but it's an over-simplification to attribute it as an underlying cause of eating disorders, which are rooted in emotional issues.

Anorexia is a condition that's notoriously hard to treat – simply because sufferers are so determined. Many women never succeed in fully shaking it off, although thankfully, by the time they reach their forties, they often manage to find a way of keeping their disorder in check. This involves a need for constant vigilance – and working out ways of dealing with emotional stress that don't involve acting out compulsions via food.

Bulimia

Bulimia is a process whereby the sufferer is locked in an endless cycle of binge eating, followed by vomiting, in an attempt to avoid putting on weight. Just like anorexia, it's usually triggered by a deep-rooted sense of low self-worth and issues around codependency. Some bulimics may only vomit occasionally, but for many it happens on multiple occasions every day.

I've met people with bulimia who will spend literally hundreds and hundreds of pounds on food every week, all of which they binge on before making themselves throw up. While they're in the act of bingeing they can experience an enormous rush of power and excitement. It's as if they experience a high through the unbridled consumption of food, often in the form of sugary things like chocolates and sweets.

In extreme cases, the urge to continue eating is so overwhelming that people have been known to throw up into rubbish bins and then scoop out their own vomit in order to eat it. You can only imagine the feelings of shame and disgust that this causes them. Ironically, these feelings in turn continue to drive the process of bingeing, because bulimics deal with the distress through more comfort eating.

Inducing vomiting is a dangerous process that robs the body of vital vitamins and electrolytes, so even though they maintain a normal weight, bulimics often encounter other medical problems. In extreme cases the sufferer can be at risk from heart attack or stroke. Some bulimics develop the ability to throw up almost at will, without the need to put their fingers down their throats. When this occurs, the sphincter at the bottom of their oesophagus may stop working correctly, and the contents of the stomach are able to leak upwards, leading to foul breath that stinks of vomit.

A bulimic's teeth become discoloured from constant contact with the acid contained in their vomit, and their cheeks become puffy and hamster-like. If a sufferer already has an addictive nature that's characterized by low self-esteem, these side effects make them feel all the more traumatized.

Self-Harming

A phenomenon that often exists alongside bulimia is overt self-harming, which may involve the sufferer deliberately cutting themselves. This is largely an attempt to substitute physical pain for emotional pain, because the former somehow feels more bearable. Typically, sufferers will cut their arms, sometimes with very deep gashes that require hospital treatment.

I've known young girls to attend treatment centres with their arms bandaged from wrist to shoulder. The girls' upper limbs are left deeply scarred, to the extent that they refuse to wear sleeveless outfits. Other forms of self-harming might include inflicting burns to arms or legs, or attempting to harm the genital area by plucking out pubic hairs.

> When somebody self-harms, the feelings they experience are very complex. The pain they feel from the act of cutting, for example, seems to release something within them, like a form of emotional blood-letting.

They describe the process as being like flushing out their negative feelings about their own self-worth and inner self-esteem. It's as if the emotional pain that they feel in their lives is so great they're willing to substitute it for the physical pain caused by self-harming. This physical pain is angry and raw – but it's easier to deal with than the emotional agony that it masks.

The correlation between bulimia and self-harming seems to exist to a greater extent than it does in anorexics or overeaters, but they too may also self-harm. The way to treat the condition is to strip away the detail of the self-harm itself and work out what it is that's causing the emotional pain that leads the sufferer to do it.

Overeating

Overeaters – and by this I mean people with serious food addictions – are also seeking to change the way they feel about themselves. In the chapter about sugar addiction, I explained the process they go through in detail. It involves gorging on food in order to experience an emotional boost. In blunt terms, it is comfort eating that has run riot.

The sufferer's weight can balloon to gigantic proportions – in some cases to the extent that they're unable to even get out of bed unaided. When this happens, there necessarily needs to be someone who is enabling them by constantly feeding them. Often this person may be a misguided parent who is suffering from emotional issues of their own.

The process of overeating works in a similar way to other forms of addiction like alcoholism. If you're an alcoholic and you feel crap or insecure, you go out and drink. Invariably this only adds to your problems, so sooner or later you repeat the process, with ever more dire results. A person who overeats feels like crap because they're overweight, so they eat even more in an attempt to comfort themselves. They know they're fat, but unlike anorexics or bulimics, they cannot develop any way of controlling their weight gain.

Overeaters think of themselves in very harsh terms and their fears about putting on even more weight become a self-fulfilling prophesy as the process continues to repeat itself.

Some people may dip in and out of problems with eating, depending on what else is going on in their lives. As a general rule of thumb, if a woman has had more than three or four different dress sizes during her adult life it can be a clue that she has issues around food, since it's clearly causing her weight to yo-yo. The same applies to men, although it may be less noticeable, as culturally, people may be less likely to comment on a man's weight.

Sadly, if someone is extremely overweight it may take many years before they're able to start to tackle the causes of their distress. This is because if a person weighs 20 stone (and is 10 stone overweight for their height) it may take many years to get them back to their normal weight.

Unfortunately, until they manage to do this it's very hard to get to grips with the emotions that are causing them to overeat, because their weight continues to be a distraction. In order to treat addiction it's necessary to strip away the addictive process and get to the raw feelings that are causing the problem.

With some forms of addiction, alcohol for example, this can be a relatively quick process. If an alcoholic stops drinking then his or her raw emotions will begin to surface relatively quickly, often within the space of a few days or weeks. People with eating disorders, however, face a slow road to recovery.

But with help and support it's possible to turn their lives around. The dietary regime they're recommended to follow usually consists of three meals a day, with the avoidance of sugar and white flour (the two 'high-octane' food ingredients that I talked about in the chapter on sugar).

Of course, not everybody who has issues around food develops a fully fledged eating disorder. In my opinion most of us probably eat too much (or too little) than is good for our health on certain occasions. If the consequences of our relationship with food become negative then it can have an extremely adverse effect on our lives.

Chapter 15

Cigarettes and Caffeine

When I work with a private treatment centre, we can usually wean people off anything, with one notable exception: nicotine. If somebody is determined to smoke it's impossible to make him or her quit, even though we may be able to help them abstain from almost anything else.

The hold that nicotine has over those of us with an addictive nature is so powerful that most addiction centres don't even bother to attempt to tackle it if there are other addictive issues going on at the same time.

When patients are admitted to an addiction ward at hospitals they find themselves in a very strict regime. Their phones are confiscated, they're not allowed books or television in their rooms, and their diet is strictly controlled. The reason for all this is that therapists need to tackle the emotions that lie beneath an addict's behaviour. Things like phones and excessive TV watching are a distraction that gets in the way of this process, which is why they're banned.

Yet, despite the austerity of the regime, patients can continue to smoke (although obviously it's frowned upon for medical reasons).

They're allowed to carry on smoking because if any treatment centre tried to force them to quit, the establishment would be empty within a week.

I know this from past experience because a clinic I worked in many years ago tried to do exactly that. When the boss of the centre attempted to ban patients (and staff) from smoking, everybody responded by threatening to walk out. It created an enormous amount of disruption, even though it was a very well-run institution.

So the treatment centre in question compromised by painting lots of little yellow 'smoking' circles in the car park. Patients were banned from smoking unless they stood in the centre of one of these circles (which were just about big enough for one person and were located ten metres apart). The idea was to prevent smokers from enjoying themselves by chatting to each other while they had a cigarette.

It didn't make any difference. Even though it was January and freezing cold at the time, people were still quite happy to stand outside in a windswept car park, as long as they got their hit of nicotine!

Why Are We Powerless Over Tobacco?

Go to any place where recovering alcoholics are congregating, and you'll see dozens of people outside, all smoking heavily. These are often people who've had the courage and tenacity to overcome major alcohol addictions, yet they remain powerless to stop themselves from ruining their health by consuming tobacco.

The reason for this is that nicotine addiction works in two distinct ways – and one of them is particularly relevant for those with wider issues surrounding addictive behaviour. Most people are aware that smoking creates a *physical dependency*. We become hooked on cigarettes as our bodies become used to the nicotine, and we physically crave more of it if we try to stop. However, most of these symptoms pass within three or four days, and certainly within a week or two when we stop. But nicotine also creates a *psychological dependency*, due to the very powerful effect that it has on our emotions.

This is true of all forms of addiction, but with nicotine the psychological effect is extremely powerful. It may surprise you to learn that I consider nicotine to have a much greater effect on our emotions than alcohol does. Nicotine acts as both a stimulant and a relaxant. As a therapist I know that nicotine pacifies our emotions (even if it stimulates our thoughts). As we have already seen, people who have an addictive nature are very sensitive to emotional stress, so the pacifying effect of nicotine is very seductive (even if people don't fully realize how it works).

Everyone understands that cigarettes are addictive in a physical sense: but we're far less aware of the characteristics of nicotine as a mood-altering drug. Of course, cigarettes don't make you slur or fall over as you stagger down the street, like you do when you're drunk or stoned (on the contrary, many people claim nicotine helps them to concentrate). And for this reason, the popular perception of nicotine is that it's not a particularly heavy drug.

In my opinion this is a misconception, because the emotional hold that nicotine has over some people is almost unbreakable.

> **Booze and drugs have a very overt effect on our mental state: they make us drunk or high. Cigarettes don't create the same peaks and troughs, but their overall long-term effect on deadening down our emotions is actually much stronger.**

I know countless recovering drug abusers, alcoholics, sex addicts, gamblers, anorexics and overeaters who've all overcome severe problems with addiction, yet they continue to smoke. This is despite them being almost evangelical about the fact they're clean with regard to other forms of addiction.

When people quit alcohol or drugs, they not only often continue to smoke, but their habit actually *increases*. Part of the problem revolves around the rituals attached to smoking. If suddenly you find yourself with lots of empty time then it's natural to search out something to do with your hands. Meanwhile, widespread bans on smoking in many public places have resulted in smokers congregating outside pubs or offices to chat, and this form of social interaction has become part of the ritual.

In my case, when I was a heavy smoker there were several 'triggers' that always led to me sparking up in a ritualistic way. If the phone rang, I would automatically light a cigarette. If somebody came to see me, the first thing I did was sit down with them and light up. These triggers can take lots of different forms. A friend told me that whenever his boss spoke to him, he would go straight outside afterwards and have a smoke!

When I quit booze I went from being a 20 a day smoker to consuming 60 a day. In this instance, I was using cigarettes as an emotional crutch to prop me up because I missed the effects that alcohol had previously had on my feelings. The moment the alcohol stopped working for me as a drug of choice – because I didn't have it – I looked for something else and nicotine was it.

I realized just how far nicotine had got me addicted when I was going out to play pool one day. I had my jacket on and I was anxiously patting my pockets because I was worried I'd forget my cigarettes. I had a full packet opened and another packet that was opened and half-full, and *two* cigarette lighters (in case one ran out of gas). This was all very well, but I was only going out for an hour! That's how hooked I was – and I realized that the hold cigarettes had over me was every bit as strong as the effects of the booze.

When I did eventually quit smoking, I went through a truly awful time. I had two beautiful Labrador dogs back then, and I can remember one particular day when I took them for a walk down by the river. I was in the process of giving up smoking and I felt very low.

The sun was sparkling on the water and the wind was gently whispering through the trees, and it should have been a perfect moment to enjoy, but all I could think about was how miserable I felt. I was virtually praying for God to take me off the Earth. The reason I felt that was because giving up smoking had brought up lots of feelings that I'd been numbing through nicotine.

> **Some people find it easier to quit smoking than others. This is partly due to physical factors, and partly due to the fact that some of us just find it almost impossible to break addiction.**

But emotionally, if like me you have an addictive nature, you're still likely to find it very tough. A lot of people find they put on weight when they quit. This was something that I experienced, because suddenly there was a void in me where the nicotine had been. I reacted by stuffing myself with sugar!

I also tried substituting expensive Havana cigars for all those cigarettes (based on the logic that I'd only smoke one per day), but within a few days I was smoking four or five Havanas in an afternoon and I'd have soon been bankrupt.

If ever there was a case of moving the deckchairs around on the *Titanic* this was it. All I was doing was swapping one addiction for another. I eventually stuck to sugar, but I was just replacing the mood-altering effects of tobacco with refined carbohydrates. I suddenly found myself eating about six Snickers bars a day. Instead of using my hands to light up, every time I experienced a trigger I was stuffing my face with chocolate. I'm a bit more controlled these days, but even now I'm partial to the odd pudding.

The Health Risks of Smoking

In any hospital waiting room you can usually spot the smokers from ten miles away. They're emaciated and coughing; they're flushed, they're often skinny and they generally look dreadful. It's terrifying that people can do that to themselves. We all know that tobacco causes lung cancer, but there are a whole raft of additional ways in which cigarettes can ravage our bodies. Smoking causes medical problems that many people are completely unaware of.

For instance, one of the serious effects is something called peripheral neuropathy, in which a combination of smoking and drinking causes damage to your nerve endings at your extremities. It can lead to terrible numbness in your hands and feet. Victims can become susceptible to gangrene and can end up being forced to have a limb amputated.

So smoking doesn't just cause diseased lungs. That's only part of it: there's an endless list of other ailments, like high blood pressure, heart disease and stroke. You don't have to be a doctor to spot a heavy smoker: it's normally written on the person's face. Long-term smokers have what I call 'an expensive face'. They look wrinkled and tired, as if they've been in a battle to survive drudgery all their life. I don't mean this in a derogatory way – I'm the first to admit that I've an expensive face of my own! The crow's feet around my eyes are the legacy of the 60 a day I was smoking while I was playing pool.

It's impossible to estimate the total cost to the UK's National Health Service of treating smoking-related conditions, but it's clearly a gargantuan figure. As I mentioned earlier, according to ASH, there are around 100,000 deaths a year from smoking, but as we have seen that's just one part of the story. What seems certain to me is that if the NHS were to provide genuine help for those who wish to quit, it would almost certainly be self-funding.

By this I mean that the cost of the treatment would be far outweighed by the cost saving from not having to treat so many smokers. Unfortunately, prescribing people nicotine patches if they've an addictive nature is unlikely to work. The answer instead lies in tackling the root cause of why some people are so sensitive to emotional distress.

Why Do we Love Caffeine?

Many ex-smokers also find themselves drinking more caffeine when they give up cigarettes. While I'm not suggesting for one moment that caffeine is a dangerous drug, it's helpful to be aware that it *is* a mood-altering substance. People often consume things like coffee or sugary treats without really thinking about why they do it.

Ask someone why they eat puddings and they'll probably just say: 'I don't know – I just like them!' What they're unlikely to say is: 'I like the effect they have on my brain chemistry, because it gives me a little buzz and improves my emotional state!'

In the case of caffeine, the effect it has on us is that of a stimulant. When we drink coffee, or other drinks that are rich in caffeine, it alters the way we feel. Most of us experience a little lift and without realizing it, we're briefly invigorated. Mostly this effect is harmless, but it's worth being aware that too much caffeine can have an adverse effect on your health.

> **If you think you're drinking too much caffeine there's a simple way to find out: just give it up for a day. If you find yourself with a fiendish headache it's probably a sign of physical withdrawal.**

According to the Mayo Clinic in America, caffeine can cause a sudden spike in blood pressure. Some doctors also believe it can lead to hypertension (high blood pressure), and there's also a suggestion that it can block a hormone that helps to keep the arteries free-flowing.

Most people agree that if they drink too much coffee it can make them feel a little bit wired, or even jittery. I'm not arguing that we should all quit coffee, but clearly, if you find yourself suddenly guzzling gallons of it as a result of 'moving the deckchairs around' while battling another addiction, then you might want to cut down a little.

Part Three

The Road
to Recovery

Chapter 16

Denial: The Enemy of the Addict

As a therapist, I've seen people who are so smashed to pieces that they literally have to be carried into a rehab centre. Their addiction has led them to the point where they're so broken, both emotionally and physically, that they can no longer function as human beings. In some cases, they've lost the will to live, and are incapable of holding a lucid conversation without turning into a jabbering wreck.

These addicts look tired and exhausted, and are often very dishevelled. They might reek of booze or vomit and shake uncontrollably. Of course, not all patients arrive in this kind of state, but those who do will require medication to help stabilize them.

You might think that someone who reaches this point would have no choice but to admit to themselves that they're an addict. Yet within a few days of being in the centre, something very strange can happen. As soon as they start to feel a little better they begin to wonder why they were admitted. If they're lucky, after a few days of treatment, and lots of rest and healthy food, the shakes subside and the sick feeling in the pit of their stomach begins to relax.

The next thing I might hear them say is that they no longer need to be there. They feel that they just had a few too many, and all they needed was a short break to get them back on the right track. In fact, the opposite is true – they're still in the grip of a very serious problem. Yet they genuinely believe that they don't have an issue with addiction, and they're keen to go back to the outside world.

This phenomenon is very puzzling, and it's called 'denial'. Denial is something that affects all addicts, particularly in the early stages of their using. An addict not only denies to others that they have a problem, but they truly *believe* that they're fine. It's a very complex psychological condition and one that can be very hard to break down.

> **In rehab circles we have an acronym which sums up the situation very well: DENIAL = Don't Even Know I Am Lying. This is very accurate because at the very heart of denial lies self-delusion.**

I've known many people who openly admit that they drink a bottle of vodka every day, yet they fervently deny they have a drinking problem. 'It's okay,' they say, 'I just enjoy drinking a lot.' Their lives and their relationships may be disintegrating all around them due to booze, yet they simply cannot see it.

When I managed a pub, I had one regular who would drink 12 pints of beer every night. He'd then go home and fall into a stupor before getting up at 6 a.m. the next day and going to work. He'd then repeat the whole sequence the next evening.

For an alcoholic, giving up booze simply doesn't seem like an option. They can't cope with the idea. Booze is life itself, and they refuse to even contemplate any form of existence without it. Yet they don't believe they're addicted and they'll swear blind that they could quit at any time, should they so choose.

The point is, they don't *want* to give up. When I meet people like this I give them a simple challenge. I tell them that if they're so sure they can give up, why don't they prove it by doing six months on the wagon without any help. If they can achieve that, then fine, I wish them every piece of luck for the future. But if they can't do it alone, perhaps they need to finally face up to the fact that they have a serious problem.

Denial is an integral part of all forms of addiction, and alcoholics aren't the only ones affected by it. Anorexics are often among those who display the strongest manifestations of denial. As I said earlier, they can look in the mirror and see a skeleton staring back at them, yet they can delude themselves that they still look fat. Whatever the using process that drives the addiction, it's usually strongest in the early stages.

Nobody knowingly chooses to behave in a way that'll result in a serious addiction, so denial is the passport that allows them to continue to drink, smoke, take drugs, run up debts or starve themselves without ever having to face up to the consequences.

Of course, all addicts are capable of telling routine lies as a way of hiding their use of substances. The boozer who says he's dry but who hides miniature bottles of vodka around the house isn't just a stereotype – his is a real and common behaviour among problem drinkers. But this is still plain old lying. Denial goes *much* deeper – it's when you actually *believe* that you don't have a problem, when in fact it's blatantly obvious that you do. It defies logic and it can be very baffling to others.

The reason why denial can become so ingrained in some addicts is because it's the coping mechanism that allows their using behaviour to continue unabated. The urge to drink or take drugs is so strong that the addict cannot afford to allow anything to get in the way of that. To admit to yourself that you have a problem means laying yourself open to the suggestion you should give up.

> **But abstinence – whether it's from booze, sex, food, or whatever – is the thing above all else that the addict wants to avoid. The feelings and emotions that are generated by their limbic system are as powerful as life and death, so they'll do anything to medicate them away.**

Addiction creates consequences that are painful and troublesome, but since giving up isn't an option, the addict simply refuses to accept that they have a problem.

Addicts Can't See they Are Powerless

Most problem drinkers, or people with other addictive issues, will have a whole raft of excuses that they use to justify their behaviour in their own minds. Typically, I hear them say things like: 'I'm not an alcoholic, because I don't drink in the morning.' Unfortunately, you can still be a raging alcoholic while avoiding booze for breakfast.

The excuses that addicts make to themselves are said in earnest, because nobody really wants to believe that they can't handle normal life. People who've experienced problems in their childhood can be in denial about the role of their parents. The reason this happens is because the alternative – that their parents were less than perfect – is too painful for them to contemplate.

The same mental process is at work in their addiction because the idea of giving up and having to deal with all those negative emotions that life throws at us is also far too painful to think about. Instead, denial operates at a subconscious level, whereby the person is convinced that they don't have a problem.

Here are some of the things that alcoholics regularly say to me when they're trying to prove they can handle their booze:

⇨ 'I don't drink every day.'

⇨ 'I just need a few drinks to relax.'

⇨ 'I don't have a problem – I just enjoy drinking.'

⇨ 'I can't be an alcoholic: I hold down a good job.'

⇨ 'I have a good home and I work hard.'

⇨ 'Everybody I know drinks the same amount as I do.'

Actually, none of these statements preclude you from being an addict, even if some of them may be true. Most alcoholics are convinced that the whole world drinks. They're probably aware on some level that they get a bit drunker than most, but the idea that booze doesn't play as central a role in most people's lives as it does in their own can come as a real shock to them.

I know lots of recovering alcoholics who, when they first go back into social situations, are amazed to see that not everyone is falling about drunk. They've simply assumed that everyone else drinks until they're hammered at the end of the night – the idea of just having one or two drinks seems rather ridiculous to them. Unfortunately, no addict will ever go into recovery until this denial is broken down, which can be a long process.

Here's the sort of conversation I regularly have with a heavy drinker. Let's call the person I'm talking to 'George'. He's sitting in front of me with a nose that's glowing a brighter red than the warning light on top of the air traffic control tower at Heathrow Airport, yet he insists he's a paragon of good health.

Me: 'So, how often do you drink?'

George: *'I only drink at weekends. I have a couple of whiskies at home on a Saturday night. It doesn't do me any harm, and I never get drunk.'*

Me: 'I see. So is it always two whiskies?'

George: *'Normally just one or two.'*

Me: 'Just one or two, never more?'

George: *'It might sometimes be three or four... it depends.'*

Me: 'It depends on what?'

George: *'On what sort of mood I'm in, and who I'm with.'*

Me: 'Okay, so these three or four whiskies, do you stop drinking after them?'

George: *'Sometimes... it depends. I might finish the bottle if I'm relaxing.'*

Me: 'Is this a full-size bottle or a half bottle?'

George: *'It depends...'*

(At this point George is starting to become a bit more defensive, so I might change tack and ask him what his wife thinks about his drinking.) The conversation might go round in circles over the course of many different discussions, until eventually it emerges that George is polishing off an enormous amount of Scotch on a daily basis. What he began by describing as one or two drinks on a Saturday night is actually a bottle a day, with sometimes more on top.

The interesting thing about George is that he'll have convinced himself that he was more or less telling the truth at the start of the conversation. What he's really trying to hide is the fact that he's powerless over what happens whenever he takes a drink. It could result in him going on a wild binge, or it might not.

Men like George have no control over what happens when they get drunk. They might be in trouble with the police, yet they'll still insist that everything is fine. Blatant denial is very typical of the way a lot of addicts behave, and it operates at a level that's entirely subconscious.

Occasionally, they may have a lucid moment – normally when they're suffering a horrendous hangover after doing something they're ashamed of – but denial comes back into play as soon as they start to feel better. A few days later, they're back to their old tricks, pouring booze down their throats like there's no tomorrow. They just can't help themselves. (Interestingly, an addict's family members can also be in denial about the scale of the problem their loved one is going through.)

In Part One we saw that addicts have no control over their addictive behaviour, and that this lack of control is the central thing they're in denial about.

> **Denial is the mechanism that addicts use to avoid facing up to the fact that they're powerless. The only thing that gets addicts into recovery is when the consequences of their addiction become unbearable.**

Only when the consequences of addiction become too painful to ignore will an addict finally face up to this powerlessness. Even then, they may not accept the full scale of their problem. Many people have come to me seeking help for cocaine or sex addiction when their lives start to implode, but they refuse to accept that their addiction can also manifest itself through other means, such as alcohol.

The fact that heavy booze abuse is nearly always a precursor to cocaine abuse, or excessive sexual behaviour, simply never crosses their mind. Heroin addicts are similar in that, even when they face up to the fact that they have a problem with the drug, they refuse to accept that they almost certainly also have an alcohol problem.

This is because most addicts tend to think of themselves as being *addicted to* a single substance, whereas in fact, as *an addict*, they're likely to be susceptible to a whole spectrum of different temptations. Their problem is that they have an *addictive nature.*

This is a condition that puts them at risk from many different forms of substance abuse or compulsive behaviour.

When a person hits rock bottom they finally experience a moment of clarity about the fact that they are an addict. They may still be in denial about the scale or exact nature of their issues, but if they can acknowledge that they're powerless over their condition it's a vital leap onto the road to recovery. This is a principle that lies at the core of the various '12-Step programmes' used by most self-help groups and private rehab centres to tackle addiction. Only when we admit to ourselves that we have no control over our addictions can we start to conquer our demons... and this involves hitting rock bottom.

Chapter 17

Hitting Rock Bottom

The last time I had a drink was on 17 September 1987. For many years prior to that I'd been what we loosely call a 'functioning alcoholic' (although in my case the label wasn't very accurate, since I wasn't functioning very well at all).

A functioning alcoholic is somebody who manages to appear relatively normal, despite being addicted to alcohol. Around 95 per cent of the people who fall within the addictive spectrum can still 'function' from day to day, regardless of whatever substance or process it is that they're addicted to.

They may work and hold down good jobs; they may live in decent homes; and they may be in long-term relationships. To an outsider they'll seem relatively okay, although if you look closely enough you can usually see the cracks. Depending on the severity of their habit, their life may consist of one long battle to patch up the problems caused by their addiction. They may function, but their life is full of behaviour that's *dysfunctional*.

Alcoholics, for example, often find themselves on an endless carousel of drinking binges, drunken arguments, lost house keys, wasted money, minor injuries, broken promises, ruined relationships and mental anguish. For these people it's an exhausting pattern and it may perpetuate itself for years, or even a lifetime.

> **Some addicts may manage to muddle through, relatively intact, while avoiding the worst of their problems, but they're never far from tipping over the edge, and they're unlikely to ever be truly at ease with themselves.**

Sometimes the severity of a person's addiction may wax and wane like the moon, increasing and decreasing depending on what else is going on in their lives. There may be short periods when they feel they're doing well in life, and that their problems are being held in abeyance, but inevitably, the chaos returns and they usually end up going in the same direction: downwards.

In my case, my addiction to booze led me to a place where I'd drunk myself to a standstill. I'd abused alcohol to the extent where I had severe gastritis, and for some reason the only things I was comfortable drinking at one point were brandy and port – that's a *bottle* of brandy and a *bottle* of port, every day.

Towards the end, even this wasn't enough to satisfy my craving for booze. I'd top-up at weekends with beer and Jack Daniels. When I needed to hide things I'd down copious amounts of vodka, even though I hated the taste of it (I thought it didn't leave a smell on my breath). I was no longer drinking because I enjoyed it – I was doing it because I didn't have any choice in the matter. I was, to be blunt, a hopeless drunk.

So, how do you go from being a lunatic who can't stop drinking, to somebody who wants to give up? It's a difficult transformation because, unfortunately, the old adage is true that an alcoholic will never get sober until he or she wants to. This will only be when the consequences of not doing so are too great to live with.

If you're an alcoholic, the thought of life without booze is incomprehensible: you'd rather die. But somehow millions of alcoholics and other addicts go successfully into recovery, which is a miracle in itself. In order to achieve this, what usually happens is that they finally hit what we call *rock bottom*.

'Rock bottom' is a phrase that you may have heard before, but there's often a lot of confusion surrounding its exact meaning in relation to addiction. Typically, people understand it to be when an addict reaches the very pit of despair: the absolute nadir from which they cannot go any lower.

To some extent this is true in an emotional sense, but every addict's rock bottom is different. It doesn't necessarily mean that they've lost everything. I've often heard it said in rehab circles that being addicted (whether it's to a substance or to a process like gambling or anorexia) is like being on an elevator that's going down towards the basement. Not everybody stays in the elevator until the final stop: some are lucky enough to get off at earlier floors.

> **Rock bottom is the point at which the emotional pain caused by the consequences of addiction becomes greater than the benefits. It's when the positives derived from the using process are outweighed by the negatives.**

You don't need to be lying in the gutter covered in your own vomit to have hit rock bottom. It's not defined by the *material* circumstances in which you find yourself: it's defined by your *emotional state*.

The Day I Hit the Pit

In my case, rock bottom began with the loss of my job, a whole year before I finally quit drinking. I was still working as a salesman in the medical industry, but boy, was my life a mess. I had three raging addictions to feed: primarily to alcohol, but I was also hooked on tranquilizers and I had a heavy cigarette habit, not to mention raging codependency.

My problems had actually begun many years earlier, during my childhood. My father had a very traditional view about how a son should be, and I didn't fit the bill. (Much later in life I realized that I was gay, although I didn't understand this at the time.) From an early age, I wrongly felt that I was somehow 'Less Than' an ordinary person. It meant that by the time I reached working age I was full of fear – and for a while, booze and pills acted as the perfect medication to temporarily fix me.

By the time I was 36 I was married with a beautiful daughter, but I was starting to seriously unravel. At work, I needed a drink just to pluck up the courage to go and see a client, so I'd furtively drive to a pub out of town to slip down a few vodkas before lunch.

I was based in The Midlands, in central England, and my head office was in South London, so I had a lot of freedom to plan my own diary. In those days there were no mobile phones, so as long as I checked in now and then by landline, the head office was blissfully unaware that my working day revolved around booze.

I managed to keep up the façade for a long time, but it reached the point when I wasn't even attempting to work anymore. I was too afraid. All I wanted to do was drink, and every part of my life suffered as a result. The guilt and shame I felt were immense.

When the phone call from my boss finally came, I knew what to expect: 'David, we'd like you to come to London. We need to have a conversation with you.'

In my heart I understood that I was going to be fired, but I decided to try and keep up the pretence for just a little longer by attempting to dry myself out. The meeting I was due to attend was in three days' time, so I had 72 hours to detox.

I went through three days of cold turkey, during which I tried to quit booze, tranquilizers and cigarettes, all at the same time. I didn't know it, but for somebody who was physically dependent on three different substances, stopping so abruptly without medical supervision was probably the worst thing to do. But for three long days I existed in a twilight world of terrifying night sweats and uncontrollable shakes.

During the drive to London I felt awful – absolutely dreadful, in fact. When I finally got to see my boss I knew what was coming and I accepted it. He was succinct and to the point: 'This isn't a good fit. What we think you should be doing and what you think you should be doing are different things. We're terminating your employment.'

Well, what *I thought* I should be doing was going to the pub every day (because I was terrified of life), so I can understand why they weren't happy!

> **I was probably drinking about a half to a full bottle of vodka at the time, with an enormous amount of extra alcohol at weekends. But, like most alcoholics, I've no real idea how much I was drinking: it was constant.**

I'd driven down to London in my company car, so the firm offered to drive me back home. During the journey I was exhausted and depressed, but even then if you'd asked me, I'd have fervently denied that I had an alcohol problem.

Being fired wasn't a shock, but what happened later that afternoon *definitely* was. When I got home my wife opened the door and asked me what was wrong. I told her I'd lost my job... and the next thing I knew I was waking up in hospital! As I'd walked into the living room I'd had a grand mal seizure brought on by the physical toll that the withdrawal from drink and drugs had taken on my body.

At the hospital, the doctor had concluded I was either an epileptic, or another factor was involved. 'When we brought you in, you had quite a high alcohol level in your blood,' he explained. And that was after three days of being dry! I opted for being an epileptic

(I'm not), because in my misguided mind it gave me an excuse for my behaviour.

The doctor put me back on tranquilizers and recommended that I didn't drink (I interpreted this as that I'd be okay if I just drank shandy). For a while I got by. But eventually I needed to find another job, and, incredible as it may seem, I decided that I wanted to run my own pub! And that's exactly what I did. I went to see a brewery and, being a salesman, I managed to convince them that I'd make a great publican. I even took part-time work in a pub to get experience.

Unfortunately, when I finally achieved my goal, it sent my anxiety levels off the scale because my real problem had always been dealing with people. As a salesman I'd had to do it two or three times a day at most – but as a landlord I had to deal with the public around the clock. It sent the stress factor from an imaginary 30 to in excess of 3,000!

So, how did I react? I drank and I drank and I drank. That's when the daily bottles of brandy and port kicked in. My physical tolerance to booze soon completely disappeared, and I started drinking beer in the mornings as a sort of 'wake me up'. I was drunk all the time, and began to have alcoholic blackouts, which are terrifying. They occur when you're lucid and awake, but you're in a kind of delirium and can't remember a thing about them afterwards.

Finally, one morning during an alcoholic blackout I threatened my cleaning lady with a knife. A doctor was called, who in turn called a psychiatrist and a social worker. The psychiatrist told me that if I refused to go to a psychiatric hospital I'd be sectioned, so I agreed to go voluntarily so I could stop off for a drink on the way.

I arrived at the hospital carrying a glass containing seven shots of brandy. After that I just cried for two days. I've never felt so bad in my life – so hopeless, and so devoid of purpose. I thought the whole world was against me.

I was in and out of that hospital for the next three months, during which time I attempted suicide twice (once seriously, and once half-heartedly to try and win sympathy). On one occasion when they let me out for a weekend, I insisted on throwing a party at the pub. I got completely wasted. I started throwing bottles of ale at the wall in order to get attention, and when the police were called I threatened to punch them. I ended up face-down and handcuffed in an ambulance, with a burly cop kneeling on my back.

Eventually, the doctors told my wife to fear the worst. My addiction to booze was going to kill me. The psychiatric hospital said they couldn't do anything else for me, and I was sent home. I was full of despair, fear, shame, guilt – and hopelessness. I was sick and tired of being *sick and tired*, and I knew the game was up.

> **My long-suffering wife would no longer support me, the doctors had endured enough and didn't want to treat me, and the police had had their fill of me too. Two days later I picked up the phone and contacted a self-help organization.**

I'd finally reached rock bottom.

As I said earlier, the circumstances of every addict's rock bottom are different, but the common factor is that it occurs when the pain caused by the addiction becomes so intense that they can no longer function as a human being. It's an experience that differs greatly from person to person – not everyone's rock bottom was as drawn out as mine was, although quite a few people will have been through an awful lot worse.

Its severity will depend on the addict's age, the amount of time they've been addicted, and the way in which the addiction manifests itself. If an alcoholic started drinking in their teens, they'll usually get to between 35 and 45 before the impact of their drinking becomes so great that they actually need to seek help – often because they've lost their marriage, their job and some of their health. They may also have crashed cars, got arrested or gone bankrupt (or been through any other similarly awful experience).

The pain of these consequences becomes so great that the person simply cannot bear to continue drinking; yet they cannot contemplate life without alcohol. It's a terrible dilemma and it causes them to collapse emotionally.

In truth, the consequences of their drinking may have been outweighing the benefits for years, but they've failed to acknowledge it (this is *denial*, which we explored earlier). Rock bottom is the moment of clarity: the point at which the addict has the cognitive ability to *finally* understand what's been happening to them – and it can be overwhelming. I've included my own story in this chapter not just to show what a horrible experience it can be, but also to show how for me, it was part of the process I had to go through in order to get better. Understanding rock bottom is important because for many addicts it's what immediately precedes going into the recovery process.

Chapter 18

The Shame Sack

Acting out our addictions can drive us to do things that we wouldn't *dream* of doing in normal circumstances. We might be the most timid person in the world when we're clean and sober, yet when we're drunk, or high on drugs, we may become a snarling ogre who rages against everything.

Addiction can take us into arguments and fights; it can lead us to crash our cars and smash up property; and it can cause us to cheat on our partners. It can make us selfish and self-centred to an unacceptable degree. Even a 'happy drunk's' behaviour will almost certainly have enormously negative consequences. Drunks and drug addicts are capable of the cruellest actions towards others, and if need be, they will lie, cheat and steal in order to feed their addictions.

This can be said of all forms of addiction, including those that are built around compulsive behaviour such as gambling, anorexia, and even self-harming. Addicts repeat these actions again and again, even though they may be aware that it's damaging to both themselves and others. This creates a very powerful emotion within them, one that I believe stands out above all others: *shame*.

By the time most addicts reach rock bottom they've been carrying around years of hidden shame. It's like a huge weight bearing down on their backs, and I call this the Shame Sack. Every time you get drunk and let someone down, every time you get smashed and cause a scene, or every time you blow your wages on some form of compulsion... it all goes into your Shame Sack.

Shame is one of the most unbearable emotions that a human can experience, which is what makes it such a dangerous one.

Guilt is when we feel bad about something that we've done wrong, but shame goes much deeper. Shame is when you feel fundamentally bad about your own value as a person.

Shame brings up anxiety, and it brings up reticence: it makes you feel as if you don't even want people to *look* at you. It's the ultimate experience of being 'Less Than'. It's a gut-wrenching sensation of worthlessness. When an addict experiences shame, the feeling it creates is so painful that they simply cannot bear it – which drives them even further towards more addictive behaviour.

If you wake up feeling like shit because of something you did the night before, then sooner or later the shame is likely to cause you to have another drink or drug – and the whole wretched cycle starts over again. These feelings of shame can lay dormant within us, stored away in our Shame Sack, continually weighing us down and eating away at our sense of self-worth.

When we hit rock bottom the feelings of remorse can be overwhelming: we no longer function adequately as a normal human being. Any alcoholic will tell you about the sense of utter despair they experience when they wake up sweating and with a thumping head, trying to patch together the events of the night before.

The shame they feel is wearying and exhausting. Every time they do something to make them feel this way, it accumulates a little bit more weight in their Shame Sack. Whenever they let themselves (and others) down with yet another drunken escapade, it adds to the emotional baggage they're carrying.

I've met men who are consumed with shame because they've cheated on their partners (whom they profess to love dearly when they're sober) and have contracted sexually transmitted diseases as a result. In some cases, their partners have become infected too, which is obviously soul-destroying.

How Shame Drives Addiction

The phenomenon of extreme sensitivity to shame isn't limited to alcoholics and drug addicts – it affects all human beings. But shame has a particularly pronounced impact on those of us who have an addictive nature. People who binge on sugary food will feel furtive and guilty afterwards. When they see the effect that it has on their body – when their weight balloons – they feel ashamed of the way they look.

> Shame is one of the most powerful drivers of addiction. It can stay locked inside us at a subconscious level, ready to manifest itself whenever we're feeling 'Less Than'.

Meanwhile, people who are addicted to sex are among those who experience the most intense shame, because of the highly intimate nature of their problem. It's also important to note that shame isn't just triggered by extreme behaviour; it can be generated by events that, to an outsider, might seem relatively trivial.

A friend of mine who spent 20 years as a suffering alcoholic got involved in some awful drunken escapades during that time, including being thrown into police cells. Yet one of the occasions that caused him the most shame was when he arrived home slightly worse for wear one evening, despite having promised to help his wife revise for a forthcoming exam. He was too fuzzy to be of any use.

It didn't matter too much in the grand scale of things – the exam was still a few week's off, so there was plenty of time to catch up. Nonetheless, the shame he felt after letting his wife down was very powerful, and it was one of the things that eventually contributed to him giving up alcohol.

Another source of secret shame for my friend was the fact that his drinking had meant he'd never made any effort to spend quality time with his niece, something he'd vowed to do when she was born. In my own case, one of the relatively minor things that caused me a lot of shame was seeing a photo of my daughter that I took by chance. It showed her peering around the door at me, clearly wondering why her dad was behaving like a drunken nut with a camera.

Of course, all this shame that we feel gets bottled up inside us and fuels more addictive behaviour, which in turn leads to even more shame. Like so many things connected to addiction, it's a self-perpetuating vicious circle.

So when someone hits rock bottom and comes into recovery, we not only have to help them stop using drink or drugs (or whatever other form of compulsive behaviour they're using), but we also have to tackle their feelings of shame. This is no easy task because in most cases, as well as carrying the fallout from years of addiction in their Shame Sack, addicts will also be carrying an enormous amount of baggage dating back to their childhood. Thankfully, treatment centres are starting to recognize this and act on it.

The One40 Group (at which I'm currently Director of Treatment) has adopted some very effective shame-reduction strategies for helping addicts come to terms with their feelings. These involve revisiting the shameful behaviour during therapy sessions in order to let go of it. This is done by non-cognitive therapy within the treatment process. By this I mean therapy that addresses the limbic (emotional) part of the brain, rather than the conscious cognitive part of our mind.

The Four Layers of Addiction

There are usually four layers to any addictive process – with each layer influenced by the one beneath it – and shame plays a key role in binding these four layers together.

As I will explain later, it's a bit like the skin of an onion. When people come into recovery in a treatment centre, it's the therapist's job to peel back each one of these layers so we can deal with the *emotional* causes of addiction.

The outer layer is the using habit itself – the addiction. This is when we drink alcohol or abuse drugs – or take part in any other form of compulsive behaviour, such as overeating or obsessive sexual practices.

Beneath addiction, we have feelings, and below that are trauma, and then sensitivity in the centre. If this seems a little abstract, it might be helpful to see it as a diagram containing concentric circles:

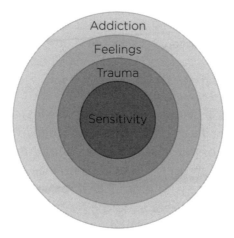

People with an addictive nature – 'The Watchers' we learned about in Chapter 5 – are those who are born with a predisposition to be super-sensitive to emotional distress. So the inner core is sensitivity.

If these people experience traumatic events (particularly if they occur during their childhood), it triggers strong feelings within them, so the second layer is trauma. These traumatic experiences create powerful emotions, which are represented by the word 'feelings' on the third layer.

If you're a 'Watcher' with an addictive nature, you're extremely sensitive to these feelings. As we've learned, they're visceral by nature and they exist in your limbic system, so you have very little cognitive control over them. The feelings become so unbearable that you seek to medicate them through drink and drugs (or anything else) in an attempt to escape them.

Shame is the main feeling that drives this process, so you can see that, in order to tackle addiction, we need to empty our Shame Sack. Of course, before we can do this, we need to stop acting out our addiction, since it's continually fuelling more and more feelings of shame.

For this reason, when somebody comes into recovery the first thing we do is take away their 'drug of choice', regardless of whether it's a substance or a process. Cutting down simply won't work, as by the time somebody hits rock bottom the situation has gone way beyond that.

If a substance like alcohol, or a drug like heroin, are involved, this often requires a period of detoxification. These substances have a very depressive effect on the central nervous system, so if they're stopped abruptly it causes a bounce effect that creates physical withdrawal symptoms. These require medical expertise to manage, so anyone who is quitting a heavy drinking habit, for example, is likely to be prescribed a drug called Librium for a few days.

Librium has a calming effect and ultimately reduces the risk of a seizure (as I mentioned earlier in this book, I suffered several grand mal fits when I tried to stop without medical help). The patient might also be given sleeping pills to help them through the initial period of withdrawal. This is because the substances they're addicted to have a sedative effect on them, and if they're suddenly removed the addict's anxiety levels can rocket.

However, managing withdrawal symptoms is usually something that doctors are able to do with reasonable confidence, especially in a controlled environment like a treatment centre. This takes away the top layer of addiction – the using habit itself. However, this is only a very small step in a much longer process.

> **Beating physical withdrawal typically takes just a few days, but what we're left with afterwards is feelings – lots and lots of them – and these are normally extremely powerful and painful.**

Since an addict's normal way of dealing with emotional distress is via their addiction, there's a strong urge to resume abusing the substance. So the bigger challenge isn't just detoxing – it's *staying* clean.

The Shame Core

A very important part of the recovery process is to let go of all the shame we've been carrying around. And the best way to deal with shame is to confront it head on. For an addict this involves a process of mental house cleaning in which we acknowledge our own part in contributing to our feelings of shame. If we've been acting out an addiction for many years, there's likely to be no shortage of baggage we'll need to unburden.

This is a very traumatic process in itself, but it's also a very natural one. In simple terms, we feel better whenever we 'get things off our chest.' Typically, my work involves speaking to patients in group sessions, during which they explore their past behaviour, and we examine the emotional distress and shame it has caused them and other people.

At this stage, patients typically find themselves in a very raw state and they can become very emotional. Through group therapy (combined with one-to-one sessions if required), it's possible for them to begin to understand the nature of the destructive process in which they've become trapped.

The overall effect of this is very cathartic, but it can take many weeks or even months to achieve. In some ways, it's akin to clearing up the wreckage caused by addiction – and there are various techniques for this which I explore in subsequent chapters.

However, this emotional wreckage – the contents of our Shame Sack – is very much just an outer layer. At the heart of the addiction lies the thing that triggered the process in the first place. This is what therapists call the Shame Core.

The Shame Core consists of the buried feelings from childhood that exist within every addict. It predates those feelings of shame that are caused by the things we do when we're drunk or smashed out of our brains on drugs.

Our Shame Core exists at the very centre of our being. It's made up of the negative feelings and emotions that were picked up during childhood, and it continues to have a huge effect on us as adults. The Shame Core exists within our limbic system, so we have very little conscious control over how it causes us to behave. The feelings of shame that are generated by addiction itself are created later on, but our Shame Core has usually been with us from an early part of our life.

In every case of addiction that I've encountered, it's the Shame Core that is at the root of the problem. This is an idea that has been pioneered by the therapist Pia Mellody, of the Meadows Clinic in Arizona, USA. I'm hugely indebted to Pia – I've been lucky enough to meet her on many occasions, and her thoughts have helped to shape my own understanding of addiction.

An addict is surrounded by shame, so not only do they need to tackle the outer circle of shame caused by the addictive process, they also need to get inside the Shame Core itself in order to achieve a lasting recovery. Their Shame Core was formed during childhood by the way that they interacted with their family or primary caregivers.

Before we can tackle the second layer of addiction – trauma – we therefore need to go back to study an addict's Family of Origin: their family background. As we will see in the next chapter, it's what makes them tick as a human being.

Chapter 19

Childhood Trauma and Family of Origin

One of the friends I made via the Priory, I'll call him John (not his real name), suffers from a bizarre affliction which, although it may sound strange, is a perfect example of how childhood trauma can still affect us as adults.

John can be sitting on the sofa feeling relaxed and happy – perhaps reading a book or watching TV – but the moment he hears the sound of his wife cleaning the dishes in the kitchen he experiences strong feelings of anger. It's not that she's overtly noisy, it's just that the sound of the dishes clattering as she loads them into the dishwasher always has an immediate effect on him.

He's overcome by feelings of severe discomfort and unease, which are quickly followed by fury and anger. It seems like a very unusual reaction, but it's very real. His typical response in this scenario is to scream at his wife: *'Shut the fuck up!'*

Understandably, John's wife considers his outbursts to be an overreaction, and they often end up having a blazing confrontation. Aside from these regular bust-ups, their marriage is in a healthy state. Other loud noises, like someone using a vacuum cleaner or a food mixer, don't seem to bother John in the same way. So what is it about the sound of clanking crockery that makes him react so strangely?

John told me about his aversion as an aside one day, during a conversation about something else. He explained that as soon as he hears dishes clattering it triggers an automatic response within him.

He feels a rush of strong emotions, which he described as a mixture of fear, dread and extreme anger. It's something over which he has no control, and it was obvious to me that it's his limbic system that's driving his reaction.

For John, it's like ducking from a baseball: something that he does without thinking, and can't stop himself from doing. He's learned to live with it and takes it for granted that any banging and clanking in the kitchen will get on his nerves. It had never occurred to him that the cause of his affliction could be rooted deep in his childhood, and that it was directly related to the fact that, for most of his adult life, he'd been an alcoholic.

John is in his late forties now and hasn't had a drink since he went into the Priory several years ago. When he went into recovery we discovered that a lot of his problems were caused by traumatic events that had occurred during his childhood.

John's parents went through a very acrimonious divorce when he was around eight years old, and prior to his father leaving home, the household had become increasingly violent as his parents engaged in a number of rows. During these confrontations his father would regularly throw plates and other crockery, which would smash into pieces – a terrifying thing for a young child to witness.

John had learned to associate the sound of clanking and crashing crockery with domestic violence – and he'd been deeply traumatized by the experience. On a number of occasions John had watched powerless as his father verbally and physically attacked his mother and then stamped around the house, shouting and smashing plates. The fear that this triggered within him was stored away by his limbic system, and from that point onwards, he had a subconscious association between the sound of clanking crockery and feelings of fear, terror and fury. It created in him a sensation of being helpless, and of being 'Less Than', which, in turn, led him to be angry and aggressive as a defence mechanism.

Forty years later, these associations are still with him – even though he has no conscious awareness of them. The whole process operates at a limbic level, and he has very little influence over it. He doesn't hear a dish clank and think: *That reminds me of when dad used to smash up the house*. Instead, he just instinctively becomes angry, and shouts at his long-suffering wife.

John has very few conscious memories of the domestic violence he witnessed – other than a few fleeting pictures in his mind – and he rarely thinks about them. However, his limbic system can remember the *feelings* in great detail – and they are triggered every time he hears crashing from the kitchen, although he doesn't know why.

> **We tend to think of our memories as pictures that are played out in our head like a movie, but in fact many of them are much more deeply rooted and they affect us on a subconscious level.**

The feelings we carry with us from childhood continue to have an enormous impact on our emotional state as adults – and addicts often remain affected by them throughout their lives. If somebody is born with a genetic predisposition to be super-sensitive to emotional distress – in other words, if they carry the 'Watcher Gene' – any childhood trauma will affect them far more adversely than would otherwise be the case.

As well as deeply traumatizing him, John's experiences also made him feel deeply ashamed. They added an enormous amount of baggage to his Shame Core within his mental Shame Sack.

Of course, it wasn't John's fault that his parents had blazing rows in front of him: he'd been an innocent child who'd played no part in their confrontations. But children are amazingly instinctive. They can sense when something is fundamentally wrong, and as a result they can inherit shame from their parents.

John's father's rages were something that the family never mentioned outside of the home: they were a dirty little secret that John was unwittingly privy to. He therefore instinctively felt ashamed about the situation (i.e., he was carrying his parents' shame).

There was a history of alcoholism in John's family, so in my opinion he's a prime example of somebody who is likely to have inherited the Watcher Gene. The trauma that he suffered during childhood was a double whammy: not only did it contribute to his feelings of shame and low self-worth, but it also meant his sensitivity to any further emotional distress was off the scale.

As an adult, John got a well-paid job in a respected profession, but his way of coping with the ups and downs of life was to become a chronic alcoholic. He was a heavy drinker for 25 years and it almost cost him his sanity.

Charting the Family of Origin

The impact of childhood experiences on addictive behaviour is so great that most private treatment centres spend a large amount of time reviewing a patient's early life, and in particular, their relationship with their 'primary caregivers'. By this we mean not only their parents and siblings, but also anybody else who may have played a significant part in their upbringing, such as grandparents or aunts and uncles. We refer to this circle of individuals as a patient's Family of Origin.

It's impossible to overstate the impact that our parents and other caregivers have on our emotional make-up. Children are like sponges, soaking up what's around them. If our parents speak with a certain accent, it's no surprise that when we grow up we speak in a similar manner. Even our choice of newspaper is often inherited from our parents.

What happens within the family unit has a huge influence over us in later life, and the coping mechanisms we develop as kids stay with us long into adulthood. (If you wish to explore this subject more fully, I strongly recommend that you read Pia Mellody's books, which are listed in Appendix 1.)

Whenever I work with a patient in order to get to the root of their addiction, in almost every case I discover issues from their Family of Origin that they've carried into adult life. There's no such thing as a perfect parent, and it's very important for me to state that the work I do with a patient isn't about trying to blame their mum or dad. Instead, it's a process of understanding what happened through adult eyes, in order to reduce any feelings of carried shame, and to reduce the impact of the trauma itself.

The walls that we build around our childhood can be very hard to break down. Interestingly, to begin with, John described his childhood as a very happy one. He hadn't been physically or verbally abused, and on the whole he felt that he'd had a reasonable upbringing. Although the impact of the trauma he'd suffered was clearly very damaging, he was very unwilling at first to acknowledge that his parents' actions may have had a negative impact on him.

The shame that we carry can be inherited from others during childhood, even when we have played no part in it. When we are young, our parents are like gods to us. We're totally reliant on them for all our love and care, and any criticism of them naturally strikes us as offensive and counterintuitive. In fact, it feels *shameful*.

Many households instinctively operate a policy of 'Don't tell anybody outside these walls what happens in this house.' So any trauma we suffer during childhood becomes furtive and shrouded in shame – even though we may have done nothing for which we should be ashamed.

Imagine for a moment that you are two years old and living with your parents. Let's suppose that every time your mum and dad enter and exit a room in the house they pause before touching the doorknob and then head-butt the door. *Bang!*

This behaviour might look very strange to an adult, but a very young child won't necessarily know any better. If, day in, day out, you observe your parents head-butting the door, after a while you might start to think that it's normal. The chances are that as soon as you're old enough to move from room to room on your own, you'll start head-butting the doors too. Within the confines of your house, your behaviour becomes accepted. But as soon as you go outside the home, it's a very different story.

Imagine now that it's your first day at school and as you enter the classroom you head-butt the door. All the other kids fall about laughing, and mock you. You'll probably feel very ashamed. But whose shame is it?

The answer is that it *belongs to your parents:* they're the ones who created it. Of course, this is a surrealistic example, but the point it makes is a very real one. Going back into our past in order to objectively review what happened to us can help to explain why we carry hidden feelings of shame. The effect of this is very cathartic.

When we empty our Shame Sack we tackle the very thing that fuels our addiction. Understanding that we're not responsible for things that happened in our childhood helps to lessen the power that the shame continues to have over us.

When a patient is in recovery, we usually invite them to fill in a document that charts their Family of Origin. The format varies from centre to centre, but generally the document lists the patient's primary caregivers and asks them to describe each person – such as their mother and father – with a series of nouns and adjectives. These are broken down into positive and negative words. For example, a patient may describe their father as 'strong' and 'dependable', but they might also describe him as 'cold' or 'distant'.

The words vary hugely from patient to patient, but the descriptions allow a therapist to look for areas of sensitivity. A dialogue then takes place between the therapist and the patient that explores more fully what happened during the latter's childhood.

This is often a very emotional experience for the patient. They can become very defensive of their parents' actions, so I reassure them that the process is one of understanding – it's not about apportioning blame. Very often people burst into tears as they're overcome by the intensity of the feelings that the process stirs up.

The patient might be asked to write down their views on the things they would've liked to have experienced during their childhood, but which they missed out on for whatever reason. For example, they might respond by saying that they wished they'd been able to go on more trips with their father, and this would trigger a conversation along these lines:

Patient: 'I'd have liked my dad to take me to the fair.'

Therapist: *'Are you saying that you were never taken by your father to the fairground? How often did your father take you out in general?'*

Patient: 'Oh, my dad didn't take me out – he was always at work. We were sent to stay with my grandparents at the weekends.'

This revelation might be the first signal to me that the patient suffered a sense of abandonment as a child, which is a very common phenomenon. It may well have been that the parent in question was acting with good intentions by packing the child off to its grandparents, but if it was something that was done at every opportunity then the child may have misread these signals. Through their eyes, the parent may have been dumping them at a time when they were hoping for love and attention.

This is a very common reaction for children to have, even if no harm is actually intended by the parent. In this respect, it's not just what happened that we're seeking to explore, but the *effect* that it had on the child's feelings.

The important thing we're trying to achieve during these sessions is to allow the patient to view what happened through the eyes of an adult (which is inevitably very different to the version they may previously have recalled only through their own eyes as a child). Seeing things from an adult perspective for the first time helps the patient to let go of the trauma they've suffered.

In many cases, addicts find it helpful to take part in a 'Trauma Reduction session' (as pioneered by Pia Mellody), during which they're asked to imagine that they are a child again. The therapist asks the addict to relive what happened, with a view to 'giving back' the shame that they feel. This is achieved by the patient imagining that their parents/other caregivers are in the room with them while they shout: '*I Give You Back Your Shame!*'

As you can imagine, these sessions are often extremely emotional, but they're also enormously therapeutic. The procedure seems to allow the patient to access their limbic system and ease some of the distress they've been carrying around with them. I've taken part in well over 200 of these sessions, and have seen that the majority of addicts find the process beneficial to their recovery.

Only when we revisit our childhood trauma, and look objectively at what happened to us, can we understand how it affected us and then learn to move on.

This shows how important it is for someone to come to terms with their history, in order to smooth the path for what lies ahead. I believe that the process has the effect of de-traumatizing the limbic system, which is key to a successful recovery.

Only by coming to terms with the demons of our past, can we learn to live with the challenges we'll face in the future. And one of the ways we can do this is through something called the 12 Steps.

Chapter 20

The 12 Steps

The first step towards recovery for any addict is to admit that they've no power over their addiction. This can be a very hard concept to grasp, since we all like to think that we're in control of our lives and that we're free to make choices that'll affect the outcome of whatever it is that we're doing.

Clearly, we all need to decide whether to get up in the morning or to turn off the alarm clock and go back to sleep. We make decisions all the time, and so admitting to ourselves that we're powerless doesn't absolve us from responsibility for our actions.

However, even though an addict might try to exert some day-to-day influence over whether or not they pick up a drink or a drug, ultimately they've no control over the fact that sooner or later they *will* revert to their addictive behaviour.

Not only that, but when they do indulge in their chosen vice, they're powerless over the outcome. Sometimes they might escape with relatively minor consequences, but on other occasions it can be traumatic.

Understanding the nature of our powerlessness around addiction is vital for making a good recovery because if we admit that we've no control, it means we're prepared to ask for help – and no addict recovers without help.

Here's a true story that illustrates the nature of powerlessness very well. Many years ago, during the period when I was drinking very heavily, an American company offered me a very good job as a salesman. They asked me if I'd be willing to set up an operation for them in the UK. I accepted, and the next thing they told me was: 'We need to train you, so we want you to come over to the US for a conference.'

At the time, I had a terrible fear of flying and would usually get totally plastered whenever I was on a plane. But I thought to myself: *Don't worry, this time it'll be different. I'll just have a few to calm my nerves and everything will be okay*.

Sadly, when it came to the big day, everything was *not* okay: far from it. I arrived at Gatwick Airport full of good intentions. I was due to fly to St Louis in Missouri before flying on to my ultimate destination in St Paul in Minneapolis. Before leaving home I'd dosed up on a considerable quantity of tranquilizers, but as I settled into my seat on the plane I was still determined to arrive in the US in good shape.

After all, I knew that my new employer would probably take a very dim view of things if I arrived with a hangover, or worse still, drunk. Then, as we were sitting on the tarmac, the cabin crew made an announcement: *'Ladies and gentlemen, we regret to inform you that, due to a dispute with cabin staff, we will not be selling alcohol on this flight...'*

My heart sank. Ten hours without a drink! Then, just as I was about to panic, they made another announcement that was music to my ears. *'However, we will be serving complimentary alcoholic drinks from the galley.'* Yippee! In my mind, everything was now going to be okay and I proceeded to help myself to large gin and tonics. You can guess the rest. I can't remember anything of the flight from about halfway across the Atlantic onwards because I got so drunk.

The next thing I knew I was waking up in a hospital bed in St Louis in the middle of the night. I was several hundred miles from my destination, and the clock was counting down to the start of the conference. I had a bloody gash across the top of my head that had four stitches in it. 'You had a bit of a fall,' was all the nurses told me. To this day I've absolutely no idea what happened, but I assume that I was so drunk I was carried off the plane and thrown out of the airport during the stopover in St Louis.

I decided to discharge myself from the hospital, but it was 4 a.m. and I didn't have a clue where I was. I didn't even have any US currency in my wallet, as I'd intended to change my British pounds upon arrival. Eventually, I made my way back to the airport, where I managed to borrow $100 from a traveller's charity in order to pay for a taxi.

I finally arrived in St Paul, a day late, and sat in the conference hall with a big plaster on my head. That evening, all the other delegates went down to the bar at the local hotel, where they mainly drank Coca-Cola. Anxious to ease my hangover, I started tucking into the Martinis and got drunk again.

I woke up the next morning with another hangover and didn't make it to the conference building until 10 a.m., two hours after everybody else had arrived. As I entered the hall I could sense everyone in the room turning towards me and wondering who this nut was who'd joined them. I felt terrible.

Amazingly, I managed to keep the job, but I'd made the worst possible start. Despite my best efforts to drink sensibly on the plane, and to make a good impression when I arrived, I'd had no control over whether or not I drank, nor over the outcome.

Stories like this are common among problem drinkers: their alcoholism often flares up at the worst possible moment. Sometimes they might manage to exercise some restraint, but it's really down to the luck of the draw. Every time you drink you're dancing with chaos and the outcome is beyond your control.

Only by eventually seeking help was I able to tackle my booze addiction, and the first step was to admit I was powerless around alcohol.

The 12-Step Recovery Programme

Most private clinics, like the One40 Group and the most effective treatment centres around the world, along with self-help fellowships, agree that the most effective method for tackling addiction is via a 12-Step recovery programme.

The exact format of the steps can vary slightly from group to group: for example, the 12 Steps used by Alcoholics Anonymous (AA) are worded slightly differently from the versions used by Narcotics Anonymous or Overeaters Anonymous. But the principles are the same. They all state that the addict must make a series of lifestyle changes that are designed to clear away the baggage from their past and enable them to live a life that's clean and honest.

At the heart of the programme is the idea that recovery involves a 'spiritual awakening' in order to reconnect with our fellow human beings while seeking guidance from a power greater than ourselves. This may seem like an abstract concept, but the steps involved are enormously practical, and most importantly of all, they work.

The first ever 12-Step programme was published in 1935 in the USA. It's inception happened almost by accident when an alcoholic stockbroker from New York called Bill Wilson met a surgeon called Dr Bob Smith in Akron, Ohio. It's a very famous story.

Bill was in town trying to salvage what was left of his career. He was worried that he would blow everything by getting drunk again, so he decided to seek out the company of a fellow alcoholic to discuss his predicament. His inquiries led him to the door of Dr Bob, and the pair sat down together and talked for many hours.

The connection the two men made had a huge impact on them both – and most importantly of all, Bill managed to avoid getting drunk. This seemingly minor event led to the creation of Alcoholics Anonymous, and the story is recorded in some detail in what's become known as *The Big Book* of AA.

It's important for me to be clear here that I'm not a spokesperson for Alcoholics Anonymous, nor am I willing to say which particular fellowships I attend, since anonymity is a strict condition.

The meeting between Bill and Dr Bob was actually a seismic moment, because it's the most famous example of an alcoholic admitting that he's powerless and reaching out for help. The idea of one alcoholic talking to another in order to work through their mutual problems has become the mainstay of group therapy – it's something that almost every leading treatment centre uses today as an effective tool for tackling addiction.

> **The reason I believe that it works so well is because when one addict talks to another addict in order to share their problems, it creates a limbic connection between them that's very spiritual. I call it 'limbic WiFi' because that's exactly what it feels like.**

When addicts are together they realize that they're not alone in their predicament, and this is greatly beneficial. Human beings are social creatures with a natural need to interact with one another. I believe that when two addicts share their troubles it can have a very calming effect on their limbic system.

The sixth sense that I spoke about earlier in the book allows them to instinctively bond with each other – the old proverb 'a trouble shared is a trouble halved' is very true. It's also a great way to empty the contents of the Shame Sack that most addicts have been carrying around with them for so long.

The 12 Steps refer to a 'higher power' and 'God' in several places, but if you're agnostic don't let this put you off. It refers to a God *of our understanding*, so this doesn't necessarily mean a strictly religious interpretation of the word.

I'm an atheist, and for me, the word God stands for 'group of drunks'. (I don't mean this disrespectfully: I genuinely believe that the higher power at work within a recovery process is the power of the group's members to help one another.)

Of course, if you have a more traditional religious understanding of God, then I fully respect that too. The point about the steps is that they're flexible to interpretation and they can work for everybody, regardless of faith or creed.

The Big Book of Alcoholics Anonymous (which I strongly urge you to read if you have a drink problem) explains the 12 Steps far more eloquently than I can, so I won't list them here. You can find them on the AA website, and you'll need to refer to them directly if you wish to follow the AA programme.

My Take on the 12 Steps

In most 12-Step programmes (not just AA's) the first few steps involve admitting that we're powerless over our addiction before coming to believe that a power greater than ourselves can help us, and then deciding to turn over our lives to the care of that power.

My personal interpretation of the first three steps is to summarize them as follows:

I CAN'T... WE CAN... LET'S DO IT!

By this I mean that step one is simply admitting that I can't beat my addictions on my own. Step two, however, is a way of saying that, together, we *can* do it, and step three is a commitment to work through the programme together to achieve our goals.

Most people choose to do the 12 Steps with the help of a 'sponsor' from a self-help fellowship, which is the way I'd recommend anybody to approach them. A sponsor is a recovering addict who helps you through your own recovery.

The subsequent steps can help to prepare us to clear the wreckage of everything that has happened to us during our addiction. This means recognizing our part in anything in the past that has caused us shame and guilt. In order to do this we need to look back over our lives, and document all the harm we've caused through our addiction by writing it down.

This can be a very intense experience as it inevitably involves going over lots of painful old ground in order to make a 'moral inventory' of ourselves. In practical terms this process involves writing things like: *'I was selfish and drank all the time, causing immense damage to my marriage.'*

Once we've done this we need to unburden all this mental baggage by sharing the information with another human being. We also ask God (as we understand the word) to remove our 'character defects'.

There are also steps that are designed to help us make amends for our past, while also maintaining a healthy lifestyle away from our addiction. Whenever possible, these amends can take a practical form. If you've harmed somebody as a result of your addiction, your sponsor might recommend that you apologize to them in person (provided this doesn't do more harm than good).

On other occasions, you might decide to make amends in a symbolic way, perhaps by making a donation to charity. This process is as much about you as it's about other people – and the best advice I can give is that your own conscience will guide you towards where you need to take practical steps to make amends.

As a general rule, if you feel bad about something you've done in the past, you need to pay attention to it and get some advice about how to lay your demons to rest. The person with whom you decide to share your wrongs is a matter of personal choice, but most people opt to do it with their sponsor. However, it's the act of *telling* another human being that's important, rather than the identity of the person you confide in. A friend of mine simply picked a contact number from a list of self-help meetings and called a stranger out of the blue!

By working through the steps, an addict experiences a great sense of unburdening. The results of making amends are very therapeutic, and the benefits to our mental wellbeing can be enormous if the process is done with belief and enthusiasm.

The overall effect of the 12 Steps amounts to a spiritual awakening, whereby the addict finally feels equipped to face up to the trials of life without having to resort to drink or drugs, or take part in any other addictive process.

The concluding steps are what I call maintenance steps, and these involve prayer and meditation. You may wonder how somebody like me, who's an atheist, can take a step that involves prayer, but for me it's simple. Prayer is simply asking for help, and since my fellow addicts are my higher power, it is them I turn to. Meditation is simply listening to the answers.

The point I'm making is that the steps are very subjective, and you can find your own way of working through them with the help of another person. They're *suggestions* for how to improve your life.

If you wish to lean more about 12-Step recovery programmes, many of the support groups listed in Appendix 2 of this book will be able to assist you. The steps may seem very strange at first glance – and some of the language is slightly dated – but I can assure you of one thing: *they really are effective*.

Note: *The 12 Steps I refer to in this chapter first appeared in the book* Alcoholics Anonymous, *published in 1935 by AA. However, nothing I've said here about the steps has been endorsed by AA; instead, the views expressed are my own personal interpretation of them.*

Chapter 21

Early Days: Avoiding Relapse

For an addict, the early days of recovery are likely to be filled with a mixture of emotions. Sometimes there's an initial sense of elation, as they feel they're finally beginning to put their troubles behind them. Life seems a lot simpler without the weight of the using process bearing down on them every day. They're likely to be in better shape physically, too, especially if they've spent some time in a treatment centre, where they'll have been fed a controlled diet and encouraged to lead a healthier lifestyle.

These early positive feelings are something that therapists call the 'pink cloud'. Not everybody experiences them, and it's important to stress that each individual's recovery follows a different path. Unfortunately, even for those who do experience the pink cloud, it's likely to be a temporary phenomenon. Sooner or later they start to experience life on life's own terms again – and that's when the problems can set in.

When we go into recovery the 'using process' of drinking or taking drugs stops. We become abstinent from whatever it was that we were doing that was exacerbating our woes. But the underlying problem of being extremely sensitive to emotional distress continues to exist. We may no longer be aggravating the situation by getting smashed every day, but it's still there.

As we learned in Chapter 18, once the medicating effect of booze or drugs is taken away we're left with a whole load of feelings, and these can be extremely difficult to deal with. We may be confronted with things that have been suppressed inside us since early childhood, and if we're not careful they can drive us nuts.

Learning to Lead a Normal Life

As a recovering addict, you're likely to experience mood swings, and sometimes you'll have no idea what's causing them. One minute you're on the pink cloud and the next you're experiencing dark thunder. The things that trigger these daily changes can be very small: a harsh word from the boss or a perceived slight from a loved one.

When this happens, there's a big temptation to start using again, and there's a danger of relapse. In the first instance you may not go straight back to your drug of choice. What can happen is that you do what I've previously referred to as 'rearranging the deckchairs on the Titanic'. Instead of reverting to your old behaviour, you seek out new ways of trying to cope with your unease.

This can be the start of a new addictive process or compulsive behaviour that can eventually lead to a full relapse. In my case, when I gave up alcohol I started consuming sugar like there was no tomorrow. What I was doing was simply substituting one addictive process for another. This is one of the main things we need to avoid while we're in early recovery and attempting to cope with normal life.

The best way of dealing with this is to get help from others. My advice is to make use of a 12-Step fellowship, and to find yourself a sponsor – preferably someone from within the fellowship who has been through the early recovery process, and who therefore understands the issues involved. They can help you navigate your way through the plethora of conflicting and confusing feelings and emotions that you'll experience.

All sponsors work in slightly different ways, but ideally they'll be someone who can share their own experiences of coping with the recovery process. In this way they can act as a mentor. They've been where you are, and hopefully your 'limbic WiFi' will connect with them in a way that'll help you to understand that you're not alone.

In addition to a sponsor, if you can afford it, I also recommend that you find a therapist with experience of working with people with addiction. Not all therapists fall into this category, so don't be afraid to ask if they have. If you've been in a treatment centre, the staff there may be able to offer you advice on how to find a therapist. Getting as much help and support as possible is vital in early recovery.

If you're working through a 12-Step programme (which in my opinion is the most effective way of staying clean) then it's suggested that you attend regular self-help meetings. In groups like AA it's recommended that you try to go to 90 meetings in 90 days. This might sound like an arduous task, but there are very good reasons for it, both practical and emotional.

It's likely that during the active stage of your addiction you spent an awful lot of time abusing your drug of choice. Apart from anything else, this will have added up to a huge amount of time, and in early recovery it's useful to have something positive to fill this void.

Staying away from your drug of choice might seem relatively easy in itself, but you'll need something else in your life to help ease the transition to normal behaviour. Going to meetings provides a structure to your day, which is something that's likely to have been subject to erratic swings in the past. Meetings are easy to find and most self-help fellowships publish booklets that advertise times and dates, broken down area by area.

Attending lots of meetings also means that you'll get to hear plenty of practical advice about how to cope with a sober lifestyle. Many people find that just being surrounded by fellow addicts is helpful. You'll find that meetings take place in rooms that are full of love and compassion. Nobody is there to judge, and the limbic connection you'll feel with your fellow addicts can be hugely beneficial because it reminds you that you're not alone.

When you're in early recovery your mental state is very fragile. It's a very delicate process and the pitfalls that can shatter it are many and varied. One area that's likely to have potential to cause problems is relationships, both new and old. For this reason, it's suggested that it's not a good idea to have a sponsor of the opposite sex (or of the same sex if you're gay), so avoid this if you can.

This is because your feelings are likely to be all over the place, and there's a temptation to rush into new relationships as a way of coping. This isn't a good idea, as these aren't likely to be built on solid foundations, and you'll only be setting yourself up for a fall later on. If you're already in a relationship, don't be too hasty to end it.

I often hear stories of alcoholics who sober up and the first thing they do is dump their partner. This is because addicts, by their nature, tend to go at things at a million miles an hour and want to fix everything in five minutes flat. But do you really want to throw away on a whim a relationship that may have lasted many years? Of course, it may well be that it's a bad relationship and that you do need to end it at some point, but when you're in early recovery you're likely to be confused about what you really want, so now isn't the time to make big decisions.

It helps to understand that you don't need to fix **everything** straight away. I always counsel caution and advise my therapy clients to avoid anything stressful in their first year of recovery. For example,

I certainly wouldn't recommend changing your job, if you have one. The recovery process can be fraught with stress, and without the booze or drugs to anaesthetize you, it's likely that you'll be feeling very raw and vulnerable.

> **In early recovery, the basic principle to try and live by is this: learn to take it easy. If you go one day at a time, day by day, you'll build a lasting recovery that'll eventually enable you to lead a normal life.**

Early recovery is a time for self-discovery, and it's important to keep a close eye on the way you're feeling. If you suddenly find yourself putting on weight because you're craving sugar, or you become obsessive about sex, ask yourself whether you're substituting one addictive process for another. If food or sex were your primary problem, are there other ways in which you're now acting out your compulsion?

Learning When to HALT

On a practical level, it's helpful to be aware that there are certain triggers that are likely to contribute to the risk of relapse. If you're feeling fatigued, uneasy or emotional about something then it may be time to halt and take stock of things. For this reason, in therapy groups we often ask patients to remember the acronym HALT, which is a widely used acronym that stands for:

Hungry

Angry

Lonely

Tired

Each of these words serves as a possible warning that you may soon be triggered back into your addictive behaviour. The times when we are hungry, angry, lonely or tired are when we're most likely to relapse. So if you're walking down the street and you feel a bit out of it, then ask yourself if any of these words apply.

If more than one applies, I'd say you're at risk. If three or more apply, then the alarm bells should be going off loud and clear and you should do something about it. You need to take action before you go off and do something strange that'll harm your recovery. If need be, ring your sponsor for advice, but here are some other helpful suggestions.

Hungry

For much of my life I didn't realize that I was hungry. I associated that empty, gnawing feeling with the need for a drink, so I'd go off and get plastered. A lot of my cravings for alcohol were in fact hunger pangs. One of the things that I now suggest to patients if they get a craving for alcohol is to go and drink a large glass of water.

Nine times out of ten, if you fill your stomach you'll feel the craving go away. Of course, eating a balanced diet and having regular meals is also very important. It's likely that in the past your addiction led you to skip meals, or to eat junk food, and these are things to try to avoid. Breakfast is really important, because if you start the day on empty then sure enough, cravings will build up that can be misconstrued as 'I need a drink' or 'I need something else.' Some people are tempted to skip breakfast because they think it will help them to lose weight, but in fact it can result in weight *gain*. The body is tricked into thinking there's a famine, so the next time you eat it stores away the calories as fat.

The best advice I can offer is to eat three meals a day, starting with a decent breakfast. I would also avoid sugar and products containing white flour wherever possible, because, as we saw in earlier chapters, these can become addictive in themselves.

Angry

If you're walking around in a temper all the time, it's a sure sign that there are complications on the way. If you find yourself feeling angry, ask yourself why. Of course, there may be a specific cause – perhaps someone said something that upset you – but very often these are only surface reasons.

As we explored earlier, with most anger, the underlying core problem is often fear. It's that nagging voice that seems to come from something sat on your shoulder: *Am I going to lose my job? Will I go bankrupt? Is my wife going to divorce me?* or *Will I get convicted of drink driving and go to prison?*

In addition, there are lots of things still likely to be lurking in our Shame Sack that can cause us fear and trepidation. In the absence of drink and drugs, one way that we subconsciously try to deal with fear is by walking around full of anger. The problem in doing this is that we're laying ourselves open to emotional fireworks. Understanding the real source of our anger can be beneficial because it helps us to work through it, rather than act on it.

If you're feeling angry I would advise you to have a warm or a cold drink to fill your stomach, and then to leave wherever you are and go for a gentle walk. It also helps if you breathe deeply and slowly, as this has a calming effect. When we shallow breathe it can add to our distress and cause panic attacks. Of course, if you have a sponsor you can call them too.

Lonely

It's worth recognizing that many addicts have probably felt an inner sense of loneliness throughout most of their lives and they've sought to alleviate it through all sorts of chemicals or processes. When you take those away, the loneliness can come to the forefront again. To some extent you may need to accept this for the time being, and learn to live with it while you're in recovery.

These feelings are not going to kill you, and if you can learn not to mind them too much it will be helpful. There's a famous scene in the film *Lawrence of Arabia* in which Lawrence puts out a burning match with his fingers. When his servant attempts to do the same he winces with the pain and complains that it hurts. 'Of course it hurts. It's the not minding that matters,' explains Lawrence.

To some extent, we have to learn not to mind that we're going to have negative feelings from time to time. Of course, that doesn't mean that there aren't practical steps that you can take if you feel lonely – the most obvious is to call your sponsor. Going to a 12-Step meeting is another obvious remedy, because you'll always find people there who are willing to listen.

Tired

Feeling tired isn't necessarily about working too hard or not getting enough sleep. It's also the tendency to go charging off like a lunatic into everything that you do. Try to keep your day simple, and don't rush around in 50 different directions. I'm terrible in this respect. On my days off, rather than taking things easy, I race from the dry-cleaners to the gym and always attempt to cram too much in instead of just relaxing.

This is why attending meetings is important in early recovery – they help to provide a structure. Although, of course, if you're hurrying from meeting to meeting this might not be the case. There's also a temptation during this time to stay up late watching television. I can still remember my sponsor asking me why I felt the need to stay up until 2 a.m. every night.

> My advice to anyone in early recovery is to try and get into a healthy routine. Go to bed as soon after 10 p.m. as you can, and try to get up at 7 a.m. Our bodies appreciate the comfort of a regular pattern and the limbic system will respond approvingly.

Many addicts will also find they benefit from medication in early recovery; I estimate that this is true in about 40 per cent of cases. This is because, underneath our addiction, there's often some form of General Anxiety Disorder mixed in with a little bit of social phobia. This is why lots of alcoholics find themselves very uneasy at social gatherings unless they have a drink to break the ice.

Not every addict needs medication, but some people cannot access good recovery without it. (Conversely, some people may need to have their medication *taken away* if it formed part of their addiction, so there's no concrete rule in this respect.) GPs are not always the best people to determine what's required. If you've been in a treatment centre I would ask their advice, or make sure that you speak to a qualified medical professional who has a detailed understanding of addiction.

You'll almost certainly also find that you need to make a number of alterations to your lifestyle, and this could include changing the way in which you socialize. If you're used to drinking with a group of friends in a pub then I think it's a very bad idea to continue going along, even if you're confident that you can stick to soft drinks.

Ask yourself if the people in the pub are friends with whom you've something in common, or just drinking acquaintances. If you do need to attend social gatherings where alcohol or other substances are being consumed then don't be afraid to leave. It's not worth the risk of staying if it makes you feel uncomfortable.

Classic Conditioning

Another challenge in early recovery is holidays. I have a friend who went away within a few weeks of getting sober. He flew to a hotel where he'd previously stayed with his wife, but he hated every moment of it because he was back in an environment in which he'd previously drunk himself senseless. Without the booze, the hotel didn't have the same allure and it made him very jittery.

In this respect, he was a bit like one of Pavlov's famous dogs that salivated at the thought of food.

For an addict, anything that's associated with their using process can fool them into wanting to go back to their old behaviour. This is what is known as 'classic conditioning' and its effect can be very powerful. It occurs when we experience something that automatically triggers a habitual response within us, and it can be a major cause of relapse.

For example, let's imagine that you're a drug user who likes to listen to loud rock music whenever you smoke strong weed. The two activities of smoking drugs and listening to rock become a habit that you regularly perform together – something that you do all of the time whenever you get high. You therefore build up a strong association between the music and the drugs.

Now let's imagine that you're just out of rehab and newly clean. You're full of good intentions, but then you decide to go to a club that plays loud rock music. Suddenly, when you hear the music, it subconsciously triggers a strong urge to smoke weed. For you, rock music and drugs have become like salt and pepper: the two go together. My guess is that if you go to the club often enough, there's a strong possibility that, sooner or later, your demons will return and you'll start smoking drugs again.

Classic conditioning is something that you need to be aware of, especially in early recovery when you are at your most vulnerable to its effects. We see classic conditioning at play all around us.

Lots of the addicts I meet tell me that it's customary in their workplace for colleagues to go for a drink together on a Friday after work. In situations like that, you'll often find that from three or four o'clock onwards everybody in the office is relaxed and in a good mood because they know a pleasurable experience is on the way. Classic conditioning results in people feeling good long before they've even knocked off work or had a drink.

When you're in recovery, there's a danger you can become swept up in this – with the result that it triggers cravings. The subsequent trip to a bar or a pub can feel like torture, as you'll sit there sipping a soft drink while everybody else is consuming alcohol. Force of habit means you'll probably feel desperate for some booze.

Learning to Cope

This is why it's important to avoid places and situations in which you would have previously acted out your addictions. Think about where and when you used booze, drugs or other addictive behaviours in the past. The more you can avoid similar situations in the future, the greater your chances of avoiding a relapse.

Keeping It in the Moment

One of the things you're likely to encounter during early recovery is a lot of background anxiety. In the past, you've been used to medicating this away through your addiction, but now that's no longer an option it means that you need to seek alternative strategies.

A powerful tool for doing this is to learn the concept of 'keeping it in the moment'. This means that, instead of letting our washing machine head get into a spin with worries about the past or the future, we concentrate instead on the here and now.

This is a form of 'mindfulness' that might seem a little hard to grasp at first. In order to achieve it, we need to be aware of our surroundings and allow ourselves to focus on what we're doing, rather than what we're *not* doing.

This could be as simple as opening your eyes to everything around you when you go for a walk (which is a great way to distract yourself if you're feeling anxious). When they're out and about, most addicts are lost in thought and often stare at the pavement. I know I certainly did this. But when I went into recovery I noticed the sound of birds singing for the first time while I was walking in the street. Until then I'd been too absorbed in my own reality to notice what was going on around me.

It's something you can try the next time you go for a walk (regardless of whether or not you're an addict). Make a conscious effort to look at the trees or the buildings around you. Look at the clouds high up in the sky and absorb your surroundings through your senses. You'll find that you soon forget about the little niggling worries you had when you first set off.

This is what's known as 'keeping it in the moment'. It's a feeling of being grounded in the present instead of panicking about the future or worrying about the past.

The benefits of learning to live in the moment can be huge. I have a friend in recovery who told me an interesting story about scuba diving. Years ago, while he was a heavy drinker, he went diving one day with a stinking hangover. He was worried that feeling ill would cause complications, but he found that once he caught sight of the seabed in all its beauty, his hangover disappeared.

Now that he no longer drinks, he finds that scuba diving has the same effect if he's suffering from anxiety. Within a few moments of getting into the water, all his apprehensive feelings vanish, because he's so absorbed by his hobby. There are two things happening here. Firstly, by concentrating on his surroundings while diving, my friend is keeping it in the moment. He's living in the here and now and concentrating on the present instead of letting his anxiety run riot.

Secondly, he's acting as if he doesn't have any worries. Learning to act *as if* you're functioning healthily (even when you might not feel it) can be a method for transforming the way you feel.

When 'As If I Am' = 'I Am'

There's a saying in fellowship circles that if you act 'as if I am', the 'as if' soon drops away to become 'I am'. Again, this might seem a bit of a strange concept, but it's grounded in common sense. You might wake up in the morning and say to yourself, *I feel like a drink today, but today I will act as if I am clean and sober*.

Chances are that by acting as if you *are* clean and sober (i.e. staying out of bars and not drinking), you will actually *become* clean and sober! Of course, this is a bit of an over-simplification, but the point is that we can change the way we feel by the way we act.

In early recovery, it's beneficial to act in a manner that's simple and positive. This might be as basic as making sure we get up early enough in the morning to enjoy a cup of tea and breakfast before we go charging off for the rest of the day. Similarly, we need to allow ourselves enough time to get properly washed and dressed, rather than just throwing on our clothes in a rush like we may have done in the past.

I often tell addicts who are in early recovery that if they feel anxious, they should spend an hour or two cleaning their home, as the simple act of housekeeping can be very calming. Paying attention to basic home hygiene and good grooming can play a positive part in recovery. In other words, by *acting* in a way that's grounded and calm, we can improve our chances of *feeling* the same way. It involves learning to be kind to ourselves. This might mean that you need to re-learn how to enjoy the simple things in life, like reading a good book or watching one of your favourite TV shows.

Our Hedonic Level

When we are abusing drugs or an addictive process we can become 'pleasure deaf.' This occurs when prolonged using makes us more and more tolerant of the high that addiction gives us and raises what is called our 'hedonic level'. This is the point that we need to hit every time we use drugs in order to feel okay. As we use more and more, this level increases as tolerance builds up.

The problem is that when we stop using our hedonic level doesn't immediately fall back to its normal place – this can take several months. The effect of this in recovery is that it can be very difficult to find things to do that make us feel content, and it's one of the reasons that we're at risk of cross-addictions to other substances or processes.

You can counteract this by trying to allow yourself the odd treat to look forward to. This doesn't mean a shopping splurge that you can't afford, or talking part in behaviour with negative consequences. Instead, it means setting aside some quality time to relax.

Make a Plan for Tomorrow

A useful tip for bringing a bit of structure to your life is to write down what you plan to do the following day. Do this just before you go to bed, and limit yourself to no more than four items. These can be anything from simple things like eating a proper breakfast, to major tasks connected to work or paying household bills. Limiting yourself to four items will help you go to bed in a relaxed frame of mind, and you won't be projecting about the following day while you're trying to get to sleep.

If you wake up with an anxious thought about something you need to do, keep a pen and paper by your bedside so you can write it down. That way your brain will be calm because you've reassured yourself that you'll be reminded of it in the morning.

Just four tasks a day adds up to 28 over the course of a week – more than enough to keep your life on an even keel.

Meditation

Another very useful tool for helping us achieve mindfulness is meditation. This involves sitting calmly and breathing slowly for 20 minutes while you empty your mind by concentrating on one thing – such as the pace of your breathing.

At first you may find it difficult to keep your mind from wandering, but with practice, meditation can become a beneficial way of relaxing. There are numerous good meditation guides available online, and many self-help fellowships also offer help and advice on the subject.

One method that I found very beneficial during my early recovery was to lay on the floor and tense every individual part of my body in sequence before relaxing it – starting with my toes and then working up towards my head and back down my arms. It was also a very good method of getting to sleep, although this isn't the point of meditation! Instead, it's about grounding ourselves in the present and achieving a feeling of peacefulness.

If you feel that practising all these strategies would result in you leading a whole new lifestyle, you'd be right. I once heard somebody in a fellowship say that recovery is easy, all you have to do is learn a totally new way of life. If this sounds daunting then it needn't, because the emphasis is on keeping things simple and taking it one day at a time. Of course, it's okay to make plans for the future, as long as it doesn't conflict with our ability to 'keep it in the moment'.

Other Help

In many treatment centres (including the One40 Group), therapists find it helpful to work with a patient in order to compile something called a CRP, which stands for Continued Recovery Plan.

The CRP looks at every aspect of their life, including relation-ships, work, education, spiritual recovery, and practical things like holidays and hobbies. The therapist then works through this with the addict in order to devise a strategy for sober living that can take into account any issues that might arise.

Everybody's CRP is slightly different, but the emphasis on leading a calm existence is universally beneficial. Many addicts find that the first year of recovery is the most difficult, but it's reassuring to know that, in most cases, things will start to get easier. No two people's paths to recovery are the same, but if you keep it simple you'll have a far better chance of long-term success.

Finally, a word about families. When we're in an addictive process, our actions can harm not just ourselves but those around us. Other members of the family are often significantly affected. Where this is the case, they may also find it useful to investigate therapy and/or attend a 12-Step fellowship for families, such Al-Anon, Families Anonymous or CODA.

Chapter 22

Long-Term Recovery:
Laying Our Demons to Rest

When we quit an addictive process it's like peeling back the layers of skin on an onion. The booze or the drugs, or whatever else it was that we were previously using, are ripped away and they're no longer available to numb our emotional distress. We're left with a whole load of raw feelings that we must learn to deal with during our recovery, without picking up an addictive substance.

Giving up booze and drugs is only the first layer of the onion. Recovery in the long term is about learning to live comfortably and contentedly in a manner that's sober and clean. It's about achieving a healthy state of mind in which we feel at ease with ourselves. For most addicts this means experiencing something that many self-help fellowships describe as a 'spiritual awakening'.

As I explained earlier, this isn't necessarily anything to do with religion (although some people do go down that path) – it's more to do with discovering a comfortable way of coexisting with the rest of the world.

We need to let go of trying to manipulate and frantically control everything around us, and instead learn to go with the flow of life in an ordered and sensible way.

It involves discovering humility and letting go of our feelings of being 'Less Than' or 'Greater Than' other people. We need to understand that no human being is perfect, and we must learn to live with our character defects without letting them dominate us. This process might mean that there are many more layers of the onion we need to peel away in order for us to continue to lead a happy life.

We may need to constantly re-examine our relationships with others, or ask ourselves whether we're contented in our job and in our day-to-day activities. If we need to make changes we should not rush at them head first, but instead take things step by step and at a slow pace.

Many people find themselves locked in a job or a career that they simply fell into, rather than seeking it out by design. In my life I've had four distinct occupations, and it's only the last one, as a therapist, that I consciously chose. The rest I just took because they happened to be there. My job in a factory, my work as a salesman, and later as a publican, all just seemed to happen by accident. At the time it felt like I was making a choice, but I was really just falling into them because nothing else was immediately available. It was only when I went into recovery that I paused for thought and really worked out what I wanted to do with the rest of my life.

Looking Ahead

One of the things that I advise clients to do is to be aware of their dreams and aspirations for the future. This can be incredibly helpful, because surprisingly few addicts have goals in life; most have no idea where they're going or why.

This is very stressful in itself. We need to ask ourselves what we want out of life and examine what it is that we think will make us truly at ease with ourselves. This isn't a straightforward process, because an addict's default position is 'ill at ease'. We're like computers that have certain settings they automatically return to.

Our default is to return to the addictive process, and it's important to understand that this urge will always remain dormant within us. The success of our recovery, in the long term, is dependent on changing these settings in a way that's sustainable and lasting.

> **One thing I encourage clients to do is to visit a big bookstore and spend an hour wandering around and making a note of anything that catches their eye. This often throws up all sorts of clues about where their true interests in life lie.**

I've treated many bankers and solicitors who discover that their great passion in life is actually gardening or photography. Some of them have changed careers as a result, although I would caution you to pause before you rush into such a big life change without giving it sufficient thought and discussing it with others.

My own journey through long-term recovery involved having to come to terms with issues regarding my sexuality. I'd grown up believing that I was heterosexual, and I had no idea that I might be gay. As a child my father had called me a pansy, and I saw homosexuality as something to be ashamed of.

It meant that I lived a lie for most of my adult life. Although I'd had one minor sexual experience with another male when I was 15, I'd dismissed it; I was in complete denial about my true sexuality. It was only when I was well into my recovery that my real feelings began to surface.

One hot afternoon I was driving through Wales with my family when we got stuck in traffic. A guy cycled by my car wearing tight shorts, and I suddenly felt a sexual charge go through me. On another occasion shortly after that, I was walking down the street when I saw a man and a woman coming towards me. I felt confused, because I fancied both of them. It was the start of a long process that eventually led me to confess to my wife that I had sexual feelings towards other guys. She told me that she'd secretly known this, having watched the way I'd been reacting for the previous three years.

I'd buried the fact that I was gay, but deep down my subconscious knew it all along. Because I wrongly saw it as something bad, I'd been walking around feeling dirty and ashamed. It fuelled my sense of worthlessness and it partly explains why I became addicted to alcohol and prescription drugs.

During recovery, you may have to face up to things about yourself that come as a surprise, or even a shock. In the long term, the process requires self-evaluation and honesty.

Now that I'm in long-term recovery I no longer feel that way, and I'm at ease with my sexuality, but it was a long time before I could be completely honest with myself. Of course, I'm not suggesting for one second that every addict has issues with their sexuality. The point I'm making is that unexpected emotions and feelings can surface at any time after you quit an addictive process.

One of the most vital ways of helping to maintain our recovery in the long term is to continue to participate in a 12-Step programme (*see chapter 20*) This is something that's of immense help on a practical level during the early days of sobriety, but in my opinion it's just as important in the later years of our journey.

By continuing to attend the meetings of a 12-Step fellowship, we can constantly remind ourselves that our default setting is that of an addict. I've been clean and sober for 25 years, but when

I see a fellow addict struggling it reminds me of where I came from, and it makes me aware of the fact that I could so easily go back.

When you've been in recovery for a while you may find it immensely helpful to sponsor a newcomer to the programme. This involves sharing your own experiences in order to guide someone else through their early days of recovery. By helping others in this way we learn humility, and it also acts as a reminder of when we were a suffering addict.

Unlocking Childhood Trauma

However, in many cases, doing a 12-Step programme in isolation may not be enough to help an addict achieve true contentment. This is particularly the case if they've experienced a high degree of trauma during their childhood. In my experience as a therapist, unresolved childhood trauma is the biggest factor in causing relapses among recovering addicts.

In cases like this, I would strongly recommend that the patient seeks professional help by undergoing a Trauma Reduction programme, as pioneered by Pia Mellody. This is a way of exploring childhood issues and learning to let go of them through therapy and discussion. In my opinion, the majority of addicts suffer from the codependency that childhood trauma creates, and it can continue to cause them emotional distress even though they're no longer involved in addictive processes.

In addition to the Trauma Reduction programmes, some therapists also try to help addicts overcome their problems via a process called Eye Movement Desensitization and Reprocessing, or EMDR. This is a form of psychotherapy that was developed by an American therapist called Francine Shapiro, who has conducted a large amount of research into post-traumatic stress disorder (PTSD).

EMDR is a way of processing the distress that we may feel due to a past trauma, so it reduces and no longer has the same hold over us.

The symptoms that many addicts suffer from are similar to those of PTSD, and I've found that EMDR is a very effective tool during my own work as a therapist. It's a process that involves a patient focusing their eyes on a bright light that moves from side to side across a device called a light-bar.

The patient's eyes move back and forth as they follow the light, during which time they concentrate their thoughts on the memory of the trauma they suffered. Their feelings of distress may have been locked in their limbic system for many years, but the EMDR process seems to ease these feelings considerably.

Experts are divided on exactly how it works, but in my opinion the movement of the eyes somehow stimulates the neural pathways in the brain to allow the limbic system to reconnect with the temporal part of the mind. This has the effect of processing the traumatic memories so they no longer have such a huge hold over us. While the science behind EMDR might not yet be fully understood, I can vouch for its success in about 60 per cent of the cases in which I have used it.

Living with Sensitivity

The reason we remain at risk of relapse during long-term recovery is that our limbic system can kick in at any time and cause us to go off the rails. We never lose our oversensitivity to emotional distress. Instead we must learn to live with it in a positive manner. This means being aware of our feelings and not seeking to numb them through substances like drink and drugs, or processes like sex and shopping.

This isn't easy, because, as we know, we cannot simply switch off our limbic system.

Earlier, I explained my theory that addicts are descended from The Watchers: people whom nature has engineered to be supersensitive to danger and stress. Even in long-term recovery, we remain highly attuned to any threat to our wellbeing, and the result is that our limbic system remains capable of causing us to react in a compulsive way.

In layman's terms, addicts are just not very good at dealing with the shit that life can throw at us. Therefore, there's always a danger that we'll revert to our old addictions, even when we're in long-term recovery.

So there may be things that are locked within our limbic system which remain dormant without our knowledge. These might surface at any time if they're triggered by external events. For example, in my case, I used to react extremely badly if someone was late for an appointment and kept me waiting. I would fly into a rage that was out of all proportion to the situation. If the person was due at 5 p.m., but didn't turn up until ten minutes past, I'd be agitated and in a foul mood.

The reason I felt like that was due to a childhood experience that had become locked in my limbic system. When I was a boy, my aunt and uncle had a small farm in the countryside and I loved going to stay with them. They would come to pick me up on a Saturday afternoon, and on this particular occasion they were due to arrive at 4 p.m. When the time came, I was ready and waiting, sat outside my house with my bag packed. But they didn't arrive.

This was in the days before mobile phones so I sat there alone, waiting for them, for five hours. I was just a small boy and I felt lonely and abandoned. It might not seem like much of a trauma through the eyes of an adult, but as a child I was distraught.

I thought that my aunt and uncle didn't love me anymore, and I got myself into a right state. In fact, they'd been unavoidably delayed and they eventually came the next day, but the emotional distress that I'd felt stayed locked in my limbic system.

In later life, the anger I experienced when people kept me waiting was a defence mechanism against the emotional pain and feelings of insecurity that it triggered from childhood. I'd feel insulted and abandoned. I had no conscious control over this reaction, and it continued to occur after I went into recovery.

It was only when I became aware of it through Trauma Reduction therapy that I began to understand the true nature of my feelings. These days I'm able to adopt a more spiritual approach: if somebody is late then I accept it's beyond my control and that it's not the end of the world.

I don't get angry anymore, although I still can't change the fact that I'm an impatient person. It's drilled into my limbic system.

It's highly likely that most addicts have a whole raft of things like this lurking in their limbic system, just waiting to be triggered. These are just as likely to surface in long-term recovery as they are at any other time.

Interestingly, I believe that this is a phenomenon that affects animals as well. A friend of mine had an Irish Red Setter dog that would go crazy whenever it saw anything large that was painted yellow, like a vehicle. The dog was a beautiful, calm animal – until it spotted something yellow, in which case it would go into a wild frenzy, howling and dashing about. My friend had no idea what caused it: I can only assume the creature once had a terrifying experience involving something that was yellow in colour!

When we've been in recovery for a long period of time it's very easy for us to become complacent. The conscious memory of the pain that we felt as a consequence of using drink or drugs can fade, and we can begin to forget the dark places our addiction led us to. I have friends who've been abstinent from alcohol for

25 years, yet one day they've gone out and suddenly decided to start drinking again. Within 24 hours they were often smashed out of their heads and right back to the same terrible state they'd found themselves in at the height of their addiction.

One man I know went to a garden party on a hot summer's day and was offered a glass of chilled wine. He'd been sober for so long he assumed that just one glass wouldn't do him any harm, so he accepted it. He suffered no immediate after-effects – but the next day he drank two bottles of vodka. His demons returned with terrifying speed.

> **When you've been in recovery for a long time it's easy to think that you're cured, but unfortunately an addict is never fully cured. Addiction is a progressive disease that's incurable – and it can also be fatal.**

The good news is that it doesn't have to be progressive, or fatal (although it can't be fully cured). We can arrest its progress and learn to live a life that's contented and fruitful. We do this by learning to live comfortably with ourselves. This means paying attention to all the basic things that we learn in early recovery, like attention to diet, exercise and rest. If we look after our bodies in this way, the mind will feel the benefits.

The Road to Relapse

One of the popular misconceptions about relapses is that they can occur at any time, out of the blue. One day we can be functioning perfectly normally in a sober fashion and then we suddenly implode for no apparent reason. This might seem to be the case when viewed from the perspective of an outsider, but relapse is actually a process that begins long before the victim picks up a drink or a drug.

There's a respected addiction expert in the USA called Terence Gorski who has conducted a large amount of research in this area. He has concluded that there are multiple stages in a relapse, which begin with seemingly innocuous events such as a change in an addict's daily routine. In my opinion, this is always the case. Relapses don't just happen spontaneously, but brew up for some time, like a coming storm. In long-term recovery we remain at high risk of relapse because it's so easy to become complacent about the little things in life if we fall into the trap of believing we're cured.

But by being mindful of the warning signals we can be on guard against slipping back into our old, bad habits. For this reason, we need to constantly reappraise our behaviour. Are our relationships with others starting to struggle? Have we become obsessed by the acquisition of sex, or money, or certain types of food? These are all factors that can be early flags that a relapse is on the way.

In long-term recovery we also need to be mindful of building up resentments against others, as these can just as easily eat away at us in sobriety as they can while we're using. In fellowship circles this is often described as avoiding 'stinking thinking'.

This covers a whole range of negative mental states, such as when we blame the way we're feeling on others, or when we can't be bothered with putting time and effort into the recovery process by attending self-help meetings or practising the suggestions contained in the 12 Steps.

> **It's important to remember that even in long-term recovery, an addict still has a Shame Sack that has the power to affect them adversely. The best way to avoid creating new feelings of shame is to lead an open and honest lifestyle.**

A friend of mine has a sponsor who described this very well by saying, 'It's about keeping my side of the street clean.' This means avoiding the temptation to fall into old patterns of behaviour that we may have practised while we were using drink or drugs.

A good acid test is that if an action or a deed makes you feel bad inside, then avoid doing it!

Values vs Actions

One way of avoiding feelings of guilt and shame is to ensure that our actions in life are in harmony with our personal values. By this I mean that, ideally, we need to conduct ourselves in a way that's in accordance with whatever we consider to be morally correct. Of course, moral viewpoints can differ from person to person, but most of us have an inherent sense of right and wrong.

When our actions conflict with our values it causes discord that leads us to feel pain and shame, which in turn can lead to relapse. If any part of your life involves 'actions' that offend your 'values', you need to change one or the other.

Normally, this involves changing our behaviour, but this is not always the case, since we may hold values that we've inherited from others that we don't actually believe in.

Here's an example of how actions might come into conflict with values. Let's say you are a recovering sex addict. One of your values might be that you consider it wrong to sleep with prostitutes. However, if your actions are that you do indeed sleep with prostitutes, you're behaving in a way that's in direct conflict with your values. And the result is that you're probably going to feel an awful lot of shame.

In this instance, most people would agree that it's probably best to change your actions and stop using hookers (I'm not seeking to make a judgement here; what matters is the addict's own sense of values, not mine.) However, there may be times when it's more appropriate to change your values rather than your actions.

Let's say you're a workaholic whose values say that you need to work seven days a week with no respite. However, when you do that, you suffer from exhaustion, and as a result it causes you severe distress. In this instance, it might be better to change your values, perhaps to something more practical like, 'I will work as hard as I can, while taking proper rest when I need to.'

It's amazing how many parts of your life you can apply this sort of test to. You will find that the more your actions are in accordance with your values, the better you'll feel.

Relapse: the Danger Signals

The key to a contented recovery is continuing to get the basic things in life right. Here are some practical headings (some of which are similar to those highlighted by Terence Gorski) that you may find helpful:

Negative Moods

Do you feel like you're going nowhere, both at work and at home? If you're feeling lethargic or demotivated it may be time to ask yourself why. If all you do with your leisure time is vegetate in front of the television you may find there's an underlying reason. Is there something that's making you unhappy or discontented? Do you neglect little jobs around the home? Are you starting to find it hard to concentrate on work matters?

When we start to let the little things slip, bigger problems often follow. The only person who can truly judge whether or not you've had a change in mental attitude is you. The important thing is to recognize it when it happens and to take action. Talk to a sponsor, and think about increasing the number of self-help meetings that you attend.

Complacency about Your Recovery

Complacency is the No. 1 enemy of the recovering addict. If you start to question whether or not you still need to attend self-help meetings, or practise the principles outlined in the 12 Steps, then it should act as a big red light. Remember: *an addict is never cured*. By avoiding putting effort into your recovery you risk returning to your default settings.

Of course, recovery isn't just about attending meetings, and you may find that you don't need to attend as many as you did in early recovery. However, regular contact with other recovering addicts is essential if you wish to be truly certain of maintaining your healthy lifestyle. Going to at least one or two meetings a week is a small price to pay for the benefits that it brings.

If you find yourself struggling to attend meetings, you could try taking on what's known as a 'service commitment'. This is when you agree to undertake a menial task at a meeting, such as making the tea or helping to sweep up afterwards. It not only teaches you humility, but it also creates an obligation to attend a set meeting each week. The key is regular attendance.

Relationships

If you scratch an addict, you'll find that under the surface he or she invariably has relationship issues. Addiction is caused by our inability to cope with life issues – and there are no greater issues than those thrown up by our personal relationships. These are not just with partners, but with other family members such as parents, siblings and children, plus work colleagues and friends.

If you suddenly find that a relationship is under strain, ask yourself why that is. Have you changed your own behaviour towards the other person? And if so, what is your role in the problems you're experiencing? If a key relationship breaks down it can be a strong trigger for relapse, so you need to be on your guard in this area. Where appropriate, don't be afraid to seek professional help. If you're struggling in a marriage or with a partner then don't rule out relationship counselling.

Healthy Eating

Having a good diet is vitally important for a recovering addict, in both the long and the short term. Are you continuing to eat three balanced meals every day, consisting of breakfast, lunch and dinner? Or have you suddenly found yourself pigging out on junk food or excessive amounts of sugar?

A change in diet can have an enormous affect on our mental wellbeing. If you've noticeably lost or gained weight then ask yourself why. Is there something going on in your life that's causing you stress and agitation? If so, don't leave it unaddressed. Deal with it by talking to somebody, such as a sponsor or a loved one. Part of being in a healthy recovery is knowing when to ask for help.

Exercise

Regular exercise is important at any age. It doesn't have to be excessive, but it's important that you have a healthy routine if you're to give your recovery the best chance of success.

Many doctors recommend at least 30 minutes of moderate exercise, three times a week. Depending on your age and physical make-up this might consist of walking or running, or perhaps a trip to the gym. The goal is to have a regular routine that you stick to in order to maintain your wellbeing.

Stress and Anxiety

Just because you're in long-term recovery, it doesn't mean that you're immune to the pressures of stress and anxiety. As a recovering addict, your default setting is to continue to have an oversensitivity to emotional distress.

If there are things going on in your life that lead to an increase in your stress levels, it's vitally important that you're aware of these and take the appropriate action. Meditation and relaxation can play a key role in recovery and their value should not be underestimated.

Anger and Irritability

Anger is a luxury that recovering addicts cannot afford. If you're walking around with a temper like a hair trigger, it's a warning signal that something isn't right. There may be things that happen to you from time to time that make you justifiably upset, and to be angry in those circumstances is a natural emotion. But if you're routinely irritable about mundane things of no real significance, there's a good chance you're heading for a fall.

At the root of anger we nearly always find fear and issues of low self-worth. These are the very emotions that fuel addictive behaviour. If you're using anger as a tool to avoid having to deal with your own feelings, I would suggest that you're in danger of relapse. We need to work through our resentments and let them go.

Achieving Serenity

A good definition of a spiritual awakening is that it's when we find a way of living that allows us to exist in a state of serenity. By this I mean that we're at peace with ourselves and with the rest of the world. It doesn't mean being in a state of euphoria. Instead, it's about feeling okay, in spite of the stresses and strains we may have to go through.

One piece of advice I can give you for achieving a spiritual awakening is to learn to be kind to yourself. Humans are imperfect creatures, so don't be too hard on yourself when you get things wrong. Addicts are notorious for being perfectionists, but the flip side is that they're highly self-critical. Many also suffer from an inner core of low self-esteem, so beating themselves up when something is less than perfect only adds to the problem.

Remember, too, that you may need to keep peeling back the layers of the onion for many years, as recovery is a constant process rather than a finite event. As you grow and mature as a human, new layers are revealed. In this respect recovery is a voyage of self-discovery. Only by constant vigilance can we ensure our demons are laid to rest.

There's a saying in therapy circles that what addicts are seeking is progress rather than perfection. It's good advice.

A big part of enjoying a successful recovery is learning to avoid black and white thinking. By this I mean that most addicts tend to see things in terms of being either good or bad, and they usually look at everything from a negative perspective rather than a positive one. But real life is rarely as clear-cut as this. When we experience a spiritual awakening we become closer to our inner self, as well as to others. We learn to look at life in a different way from the manner in which we did while we were in active addiction.

Instead of being consumed by anger and resentment, we need to look for the good in other people, and be willing to give them the benefit of the doubt. During our addiction, we become self-centered because the fear that we're carrying inside us makes us selfish. But when the fear is taken away it should allow us to realize that there are other human beings on the planet beside ourselves.

This involves a certain amount of humility, which is something that's very hard to learn. By becoming more humble we learn to think of others. We need to reconnect with the rest of the human race in a way that allows intimacy in the appropriate circumstances.

By this I mean that we should allow ourselves to be honest with others about the way we feel. But most addicts hate intimacy. Many will describe feeling awkward and insecure at social gatherings if they're unable to indulge in their addiction. Getting off their heads on booze or drugs is a way of giving themselves false confidence, while also avoiding being open and honest.

But learning to allow others to see the real person inside us is a form of intimacy that's hugely beneficial to our recovery. I pretended to be somebody I wasn't for many years and I paid a heavy price.

A spiritual awakening also involves learning not to drive yourself up the wall about things that you can't change. When I was in active addiction I'd go into a wild fury if I disagreed with things that people said. I'd bawl and shout because I wanted the world to be organized the way I wanted it to be. All I succeeded in doing was driving myself into a frenzy, which gave me the perfect excuse to drink even more.

Today I've learned to accept that there are certain things about the world that I don't agree with. Acceptance of who we are and acceptance of our limitations can play a very positive role in long-term recovery. It's the key to finding true serenity.

Part Four

The Challenges Ahead

Chapter 23

Has Modern Life Led to More Addiction?

It's tempting to think that the widespread drug abuse and other forms of addiction we see today are a modern phenomenon. It's easy to imagine that a tidal wave of recreational drugs suddenly washed onto the streets of Western nations like Britain and the USA during the second half of the 20th century, and continues to swell to this day.

However, while it's true that certain substances such as cocaine and heroin (not to mention sugary food) have become more readily available in the last 30 or 40 years, I suspect that the disease of addiction has been around for far longer than we realize. In fact, there's evidence to suggest that mankind has been quietly getting smashed, one way or another, for thousands of years.

The production of alcoholic beverages dates back at least as far as the Neolithic period (9000–2000 BCE), and is common in many cultures. The ancient Egyptians are thought to have been keen brewers who enjoyed consuming alcohol (no doubt sometimes to excess), and the Bible contains numerous references to drunkenness, including a passage that warns:

'For the drunkard and the glutton shall come to poverty: and drowsiness shall clothe a man with rags.' (*Proverbs 23:21*)

Historical accounts show that alcoholism was widespread among London's population during the 18th century – the average consumption of gin was around two pints per week a head (a problem which led the authorities to license spirits in the 1750s).

Similarly, drug abuse isn't confined to modern times. During the 15th century, opium was consumed recreationally in China, and the substance was eventually banned there in 1729. And, since prostitution is known as the 'oldest profession', it seems a reasonable assumption that sex addiction has been around for far longer than we might think.

New and Dangerous

So, it seems likely that addiction is an age-old disease, but is the perceived rise in the number of people who suffer from its many and varied forms somehow a reflection of our modern way of living? Or have we simply become more aware of the problem? In my opinion, an answer can be given by making two points.

Firstly, I believe that people are no more addictive by nature today than they would have been thousands of years ago. Indeed, since modern-day addicts are those whom I consider the descendants of The Watchers (*see Chapter 5*), I believe the underlying condition is nearly as old as mankind.

However, the second point is that modern life has nonetheless created numerous outlets for addiction that are new and dangerous. This has been caused by factors such as the impact of technology, growing levels of affluence, and the erosion of social bonds such as the family and religion. As a result, I believe that those of us who are born with an addictive nature need to be on our guard against a far greater range of temptations than ever before.

History tells us that human beings have always been susceptible to certain forms of addiction. It's an illness that can manifest itself in so many different ways, so I believe it may have been misdiagnosed as other things in the past. While it might have been obvious if a person drank himself to death during a huge binge, in many cases lifestyle factors such as chronic alcoholism may have been overlooked as a cause of death.

This is because addiction is a primary condition that leads to other health problems that may be easier for doctors to spot. Alcohol abuse can cause all sorts of medical complications, such as heart and liver disease, high blood pressure and diabetes. In days gone by these may have been recorded as the immediate cause of death, without anybody necessarily making a connection with alcohol.

Similarly, in Victorian times, if a woman had died from an addiction-based eating disorder I very much doubt it would have been recorded on the death certificate as anorexia. There simply wasn't the medical knowledge at the time to make an accurate diagnosis, and instead it may have been recorded as a catch-all condition such as a 'wasting disease' or 'consumption'.

> **It's only in modern times that we're slowly beginning to understand the true scale of how addiction impacts on the population – and even now our knowledge is sketchy.**

What we do know for certain today is that addiction is widespread, and it has an enormous negative impact on public health. According to the National Survey on Drug Use and Health (NSDUH) in the USA, over the course of one month in 2011 an estimated 22.5 million Americans used an illicit drug or abused a psychotherapeutic medication (such as a pain reliever, stimulant or tranquilizer).[13]

This figure equates to 8.7 per cent of the population and represents a slight increase from 8.3 per cent in 2002. Most of this rise was due to an increase in the use of marijuana. Rates of alcohol abuse in the USA declined very slightly over the same period, with 16.7 million Americans (6.5 per cent of the population) either dependent on alcohol or experiencing problems due to alcohol abuse in 2011.

These statistics represent a mountain of misery and health problems, but they only provide a brief snapshot, since they don't take into account other forms of addiction.

In the UK, the official figures suggest there has been a large increase in both problem drinking and morbid obesity over the last decade. According to government figures, in 2012 there were 178,247 prescriptions issued for drugs to treat alcohol dependency.[14] This is an increase of 73 per cent on the 2003 figure.

There were also 1.2 million hospital admissions due to booze consumption resulting in an alcohol-related injury or disease (this is more than twice as many as during 2002/2003, although adjusted figures due to changes in counting estimate the rise to be around 51 per cent).

These alcohol figures don't surprise me in the least, since in the UK it has now become socially acceptable to deliberately go out and get so plastered that you don't know what day it is! A generation or two ago this simply wasn't the case. When I was a teenager, heavy drinking was common, but nonetheless the idea of getting so drunk that you couldn't walk was considered a sign of weakness.

Meanwhile, the medical profession is so worried about obesity that some doctors now refer to sugar as 'the new tobacco' because of its harmful effect on health when consumed in excess. In January 2014, the UK pressure group Action on Sugar called on the government and the food industry to take steps to limit sugar intake.

The availability of cheap, sugar-laden food means that we're now at more risk of food addiction than at any other time in history.

Growing levels of affluence in the Western world mean that we can now afford to gorge ourselves on sugar without it being a financial burden. During the postwar years in the UK there simply wasn't enough food to go around for this to be the case.

The challenge thrown up by population growth has created a situation where we now consume mountains of refined carbohydrates because they are easier and cheaper to produce than other types of food. We cannot feed the world if we rely only on protein. Modern life has therefore found a way of feeding the population, but unfortunately the result is highly addictive.

At the same time, a whole industry has been created that's devoted to selling high-sugar, carbohydrate-rich food on a mass scale. Whenever we switch on the TV we're bombarded with slick advertising that constantly reinforces the message that it's okay to consume large quantities of products like sweetened fizzy drinks. In supermarkets there are clever deals like multipack offers and 'Buy One Get One Free' (quaintly known in the industry as BOGOF), which appeal to our addictive nature.

In addition, stores often cut the price of alcoholic drinks in a bid to attract more customers. If you're going to buy yourself a cheap 12-pack of beer to drink on the sofa while you watch *The X Factor*, or some other favourite show, the chances are that you'll take advantage of the snacks the store has to offer too.

For the first time in history, most of the population of the West can eat until they're completely satiated, every day. Ironically, though, it's possible that the poorest sections of society are adversely affected by this, since there's some evidence to suggest that obesity is particularly prevalent among those on low incomes (who are more likely to encounter problems in their lives that they seek to alleviate).

Modern Addictions

As many commentators before me have pointed out, the human body has not evolved to cope with this development. Nature has engineered us to be hunter-gatherers who are motivated by a degree of hunger to exercise while we gather or hunt for food. We're simply not designed to be full all of the time, having stuffed our faces on an epic scale.

We live in a society in which almost everything we do is geared towards instant gratification. We believe that we have the right to consume whatever we want, whenever we want it. In a supermarket we expect to find all the goods we could possibly desire – all lined up, ready to buy. And for an addict, this is like throwing petrol on the fire.

Meanwhile, the internet gives us round-the-clock access to almost every product or service known to man. With a few clicks of a mouse it's possible to find everything from weather reports to graphic sex. We expect our entertainment – from video games to music and movies – to be available for instant streaming.

Computer games are an example of this. They seem harmless and fun, and you can understand why a parent would rather their child was safe in his bedroom in front of a screen than out on the streets where hidden dangers might lurk. Unfortunately, computer gaming is highly addictive. If you're uncomfortable in the real world they offer a form of escapism to a digital world in which your feelings of being inadequate are replaced by false self-esteem. The game becomes all important and nothing else matters.

I'm aware of cases of 16-year-old boys who will play for up to 12 hours at a time. It leaves them tired and listless and unable to function properly in the real world. They lose the ability to form personal relationships, and in extreme cases they don't even eat properly. I've also known gaming addiction to affect men in their thirties, who often have parallel addictions to internet pornography.

Today's technology allows us to be bombarded with new temptations on a daily basis. The combined effect of all this has created new outlets for addictive behaviour that simply didn't exist a generation ago.

The web is awash with sexual content and it's not uncommon for porn addicts to spend hour after hour searching for material of an increasingly extreme nature. In the end their habit becomes all-consuming and it can dominate their lives. Similarly, it's now possible to gamble around the clock in many parts of the world via the internet. What would once have involved a trip to a bookmaker, is now freely available in a millisecond.

Technology also impacts on us in ways that are very subtle, but which can still activate the addict within us. Social networking sites like Facebook and Instagram are often used to portray a gloss-coated world in which everybody is having a great time. But if you're feeling down and low, the effect of being bombarded with messages about how well everybody else is doing is likely to make you feel all the more inadequate and 'Less Than' others. Trying to reply to all these messages while pretending to be upbeat is in itself a demoralizing process.

The advent of smartphones has given us access to email and text services around the clock, with no respite. If you're a Watcher who is constantly alert to danger or bad news, there's no longer any downtime to relax. You're always on guard against that phone call or message that's going to ruin your day. Of course, you could switch off your phone, but that only leads to more worry because you're out of touch. It's a vicious circle.

Family and Religion

These new challenges that addicts face have coincided with a change in cultural factors such as the importance of family and religion. In the past these may have acted as brakes on addictive behaviour, whereas today they often play a lesser role in our lives. This is particularly so in the UK, where divorce rates have rocketed and church attendances have fallen.

The reason why I believe this is significant is that addiction is a disease that's isolationist by nature. When we're alone and estranged from others we're at our most vulnerable. In contrast, a loving family can give us a sense of security and warmth that's very comforting (although, of course, dysfunctional family ties can have the opposite effect). Family bonds may also reinforce the idea that certain types of behaviour, like illicit drug taking or excessive alcohol abuse, are unacceptable.

Similarly, although I'm an atheist myself, I can fully understand how religion can create a spiritual sense of wellbeing that's very comforting to potential addicts. If this means you're less likely to be consumed by your addictive demons then I fully applaud that.

As I pointed out earlier, most self-help groups describe addiction as a 'spiritual' illness, and one way of interpreting spirituality is that it's an inner sense of serenity that comes through being at peace with the world around us and having a limbic connection with the people within it.

If religious ties and family bonds can help some addicts to achieve this, it can only be a good thing. Having said that, both family and religion can just as easily be aggravating factors, so I don't want to overstate their importance. However, the fact that these elements have less of an impact on some people's lives may have contributed to a culture in which, in some circles, it's socially acceptable to drink heavily and take drugs.

Meanwhile, we've become obsessed with the Culture of Celebrity, and our media outlets saturate us with gossip about the ever-changing roster of famous actors, singers, dancers, models and reality-show stars we find so fascinating. This creates its own pressures because it's crazy to assume that we can all afford to wear designer clothes and live like the rich and famous. (Ironically, I suspect that a lot of products from designer brands are actually purchased by people who are neither rich nor famous, they just believe the hype.)

When we're unable to do so it can fuel our inner feelings of inadequacy, causing us to seek out alternatives that are addictive and damaging. Similarly, advertising creates a view of the world in which everybody must drive an expensive car or have the latest gadget. If you're born with an addictive nature, there's a danger you'll react to this by feeling worthless and 'Less Than' when you can't afford these things.

Of course, our modern lifestyle can't be blamed for everything. I believe addicts are born that way and then shaped by their experiences in life. What the modern world does throw up, however, are newer and greater temptations, combined with a culture that celebrates indulgence.

Chapter 24

Why Do Doctors Get It Wrong?

I have a friend who started to binge drink when he was in his teens. It was a problem that stayed with him throughout his university years and it led him into all sorts of drunken scrapes. He didn't care too much about the chaos his drinking caused and when he reached his twenties he decided to settle down and get married. But, despite having a steady relationship and a good job as a journalist, he continued to binge drink.

Even though he drank most days, in his mind things were okay because on the whole he enjoyed booze and he only tended to get really drunk at weekends or on special occasions. The trouble was that his definition of a 'special occasion' got broader and broader, until eventually, even going for a 'quiet' drink after work with a friend would result in him getting completely hammered.

When his wife first suggested to him that he might be an alcoholic he was horrified. But, deep down, he knew something was probably not right and he agreed to go and see his family doctor. For any alcoholic, seeking help for the first time is a huge step, because no drinker likes to admit that they have a problem.

'I'm a bit worried about how much I drink,' my friend told his GP. 'I don't do it all the time, but occasionally I go over the top and get very drunk.'

The doctor listened patiently for a few moments before asking my friend exactly how many drinks he'd have. 'Normally only two or three pints of beer,' he replied (which was a bit of an understatement to say the least), 'but every now and then I drink more and end up with such a terrible hangover that I can't function.'

'How much have you had to drink when you get these hangovers?' asked the doctor.

'About eight pints of beer... but it could be as many as 12 or 13. I lose count,' was the reply.

Now, if a patient had confided in me in the same way during a therapy session, by this stage the alarm bells would be ringing loud and clear. But then I'm not a doctor – I'm an addiction therapist.

The GP asked my friend a few more questions about his general health. He felt fine, he replied (after all, he was still only in his mid twenties, so the booze hadn't yet taken its full toll on his body). After a while the GP had heard enough.

'My advice to you is to cut out the 12- or 13-pint sessions, because they don't do anybody any good,' he said. 'The other thing you might like to do is switch to drinking red wine. You'll drink it more slowly, and you might find you don't finish the bottle.'

And that was it! No advice about seeking specialized help. No detailed investigation into what it was that was making my friend drink. No real understanding that the young man sitting in front of him was already in the early stages of a violent addiction that would stay with him for life. All that my friend received was a well-intentioned plea to cut down, along with some perverse advice about switching to a different form of alcohol.

The reason I mention this case is that I've heard so many similar tales over the years about the lack of understanding that many doctors demonstrate when it comes to addiction. In my friend's case, he was displaying no obvious symptoms of ill health as a result of his drinking, so in the doctor's mind the problem wasn't serious. My friend drank heavily for another 15 years before ending up in the Priory. His problem progressed to the point where it nearly cost him his job, his marriage and his mental health.

My own experience with doctors was little better. One medical practitioner told my wife that he thought there was little hope for me. When I finally went into recovery, I told him that I'd started to attend a 12-Step fellowship and that it seemed to be helping me. 'They're a little bit evangelical aren't they?' he sniffed, referring to the group that I'd joined. It was obvious to me that my problem was so far beyond his comprehension that I was wasting my time talking to him (in fact, I felt like landing a punch on him!)

Mistaking Symptoms for Causes

So why do doctors get it so wrong? In a nutshell, it's because they tend to be fixated on treating the *symptoms* of addiction rather than the *causes* of the condition. Another factor is that the training they receive for dealing with addiction is often woefully inadequate. A friend of mine is a qualified doctor in his fifties who now runs a successful addiction centre. One day, he confided to me that when he was training to be a junior doctor he spent just one hour studying the causes of addiction.

Of course, the situation may have improved slightly today, and I'm not trying to suggest that every doctor is ignorant (in fact, there are some excellent physicians out there). What I can say, however, is that I've met hundreds of addicts with similar stories about how they've been misunderstood, misdiagnosed or simply ignored by their doctors.

This is because doctors almost always look at symptoms and confuse them with causes. For example, if you drink heavily you might be red-faced, sweaty and anxious. Your doctor sees this and thinks, *I know what it is – this patient has been drinking heavily*. That may be true, but what the doctor doesn't understand is that the heavy drinking itself is also just a symptom. The primary cause of the patient's discomfort is the thing that's making him or her drink heavily.

It's our inability to cope with our extreme sensitivity to emotional distress that causes us to drink or to take drugs, or to overindulge in things like food or sex. This is the condition that doctors fail to treat.

> **If an alcoholic goes to a doctor, the chances
> are that they will offer advice and medication
> that's designed to help a patient cut down
> on their alcohol intake. This is all well and
> good, but when you take away the alcohol, the
> patient is still left with the underlying issue.**

This is why so many addicts relapse when nothing is done to tackle the emotional and spiritual causes of their illness.

Fortunately, things are slowly changing for the better. In the UK, the NHS website now lists Alcoholics Anonymous as a potential source of help and advice for alcoholics. In the USA, physicians are also becoming more open-minded, and in some quarters there's now wide acceptance that addiction is a primary illness that results in many different forms of behaviour.

The implications of this are profound. Ultimately, it means that in addition to managing various symptoms that differ from person to person, we need to regard alcoholics, drug addicts, sex addicts, overeaters and people displaying various other forms of compulsive behaviour as all belonging to the same group.

This is something that's already widely understood in the private practices in which I've worked. In the Priory, and at the One40 Group, it's common for people suffering from many different forms of addiction (including anorexics and self-harmers, where appropriate) to join the same group therapy sessions.

The more we understand about addiction, the more we realize that very few people display only a single addictive trait. Instead, their addictive nature will often present itself in multiple ways.

For example, almost every cocaine user that I know is also a heavy drinker. They may also have issues around sex. Quite often they may seek help for cocaine addiction, but it's the alcohol that triggers their drug use, which in turn leads to them seeking out prostitutes.

All three activities are just symptoms of the same underlying problem, the origins of which reside in their limbic system and are often characterized by oversensitivity to emotional distress and childhood trauma.

When an addict walks into a doctor's surgery the chances are that they will be less than honest about their problem. The furtive nature of addiction often results in patients being defensive and cagey. No alcoholic likes the idea of giving up booze, so they're likely to lie about the scale of their intake.

To be fair to GPs, this makes their task all the more difficult because they can only treat what's presented to them. If a patient lies about the nature of their habit, most doctors in busy NHS surgeries in the UK don't have the time to make a detailed investigation to check if they're telling the truth.

The situation is made all the more complex by the fact that the addict himself often doesn't have a clue what's wrong with him. All he or she knows is that they feel like shit, and that in some way their addiction may be to blame. In fact, what's really happening when they walk into the surgery – even though they might not know it – is that they're making a cry for help because they cannot cope with life.

The trouble is that most doctors are not geared up to help us cope with life. What they love to do instead is treat our symptoms, because that's what they're trained to do.

Tackling Addiction at its Root

The way that the NHS treats heroin abusers in the UK is a prime example of how conventional medicine gets it wrong when it comes to treating addiction. When somebody seeks help for heroin addiction, the immediate goal of the doctor is to persuade the patient to stop taking the drug, and the way they do this is by prescribing methadone as a substitute.

As I said earlier, this is crazy. Methadone isn't only addictive but it also has a lower tolerance level than heroin. By making methadone widely available to addicts, doctors are condemning their patients to years of misery. In my opinion it would be far more effective to wean people off heroin by prescribing heroin itself in smaller and smaller doses, but doctors are forbidden from doing this because heroin is illegal.

The logic behind doctors prescribing methadone is perverse; it goes like this:

Problem: Patient is addicted to heroin.

Solution: Give them methadone instead.

Result: Hey Presto! No more heroin addiction.

In reality, the patient is still hopelessly addicted to a dangerous drug, and in the meantime nothing has been done to treat the emotional and spiritual problem that triggered their addiction.

I strongly believe that it's time to decriminalize heroin so that doctors can use it in a controlled way for the treatment of addiction. In fact, I believe that in future we may need to have an open mind about decriminalizing all forms of drugs. Before I'm deafened by the inevitable howls of protest, we need to ask ourselves a very simple question: is our current policy of criminalizing drugs working? By almost any yardstick you care to mention the answer is 'No'.

All we have done is created a sub-culture in which organized crime makes millions from the supply of illegal drugs. At the same time we've demonized addicts themselves by making them liable for criminal prosecution for possession.

> **Instead of providing effective treatment for drug addicts, society on the whole has chosen to deal with them through the criminal justice system.**

Of course, I'm not suggesting for one moment that all drugs should be freely available – there's a big difference between decriminalization (with appropriate safeguards) and full legalization. Nor am I suggesting that addicts shouldn't be prosecuted if they commit a crime – clearly they should.

However, I would certainly be in favour of decriminalizing possession of most substances in small amounts. This is because we need to stop treating addicts as criminals simply because they suffer from a medical condition. Meanwhile, doctors who specialize in the treatment of addiction should have the freedom to prescribe whatever substance is clinically required.

Our current drugs laws are perverse to say the least. Why, for example, is marijuana generally considered to be less serious than many other drugs? I'd like to attack the idea that cannabis doesn't kill. Of course, it might be extremely rare for it to have *directly* resulted in anybody's death, but I've met hundreds of addicts who've come in for treatment for cocaine and heroin who all began by smoking cannabis.

Meanwhile, two of the most dangerous drugs of all – alcohol and nicotine – are legal. It shows that our whole approach to substance abuse is muddled and confused. Locking up addicts for abusing one substance, while letting them freely consume others, simply isn't working.

So, what steps could the medical profession take in order to provide better care and treatment for people suffering from addiction? I believe the answer lies in providing a response that acknowledges that addictive *behaviour* is caused by an underlying disorder of the limbic system. We need to examine and tackle the emotional and mental causes of the condition.

In specialist private practices, we regularly see positive results from tackling these through group therapy and trauma reduction work. This is especially the case when childhood trauma is a major factor. None of this is easy – but all of it is possible to do.

What would this mean in practical terms for people like the friend I mentioned earlier who went to see his GP about his booze binges? Well, if he'd been referred to the correct specialist at the time, instead of being packed off to drink red wine, it might have led to him coming to terms with the reasons *why* he drank heavily far sooner.

He eventually achieved sobriety after going into private rehab at the age of 42, and later underwent a number of child trauma reduction sessions. This was all paid for by private medical insurance. He's now teetotal and leads a more normal life. He's still an addict by nature, but the understanding that he has of his condition brings him a degree of serenity that was previously lacking.

Providing effective treatment for addicts is expensive, but it would save society money in the long run. It would take many millions of pounds of public money, but if you consider the huge cost to society from the health problems currently caused by addiction, coupled with the social and real costs of the crime that it generates, it makes sense to tackle the problem at its root.

What we require is a fresh start that's led by government and involves inter-agency cooperation from both the medical profession and the criminal justice system. Unfortunately, because this would need a government brave enough to invest huge resources, it may be a long time coming.

I fear that, in the meantime, our society will continue to simply muddle its way through, and that's a crying shame. I believe that the way in which addicts are currently treated represents a fundamental abdication of government's responsibility to protect the welfare of a huge part of the population.

Conclusion

The Human Condition

When Princess Diana died in a car crash in 1997 it gave the British nation a sudden and unexpected shock. The public awoke one Sunday morning to be told the terrible news that the princess had been killed in tragic circumstances overnight. Diana was young and glamorous, and millions of people adored her – so it was understandable that the tragedy caused a great degree of sadness.

In fact, the resulting outpouring of emotion went way beyond our normal reaction to a news event. It had a profound effect that has rarely been seen in times of peace. Suddenly, it seemed as if the whole country was united in grief.

I can remember exactly where I was when I heard the news of her death. I was in my car on the way to a shop when I switched on the radio. I felt devastated, because like a lot of people, I'd followed Diana's trials and tribulations through the eyes of the media, and as a result I felt as if I had strong empathy with her.

What happened next was quite extraordinary.

I remember going to visit Diana's former home, Kensington Palace, with a friend and seeing a great sea of flowers in the building's grounds and in the surrounding streets. Everywhere you looked people were grieving, and a wave of raw emotion seemed to ripple through much of the population. Like everybody else I found myself getting caught up in the moment, despite the fact that I'd never met Diana and her death had no direct impact on my own life.

Understanding Our Need to Flock Together

So, why did the death of one person have such a universal effect? I believe that what we experienced as a nation was a kind of limbic bonding. We were literally united by our common emotions. There was a shared feeling of sadness that transcended our normal reaction to current events. We sensed the feelings of sadness in others, and we felt compelled to experience similar emotions.

A similar thing happened in the USA after the terrorist attacks of 9/11. A sudden and shocking series of events united the nation in grief and it led to some amazing stories of courage and compassion. Suddenly, the country's petty internal differences were forgotten while people struggled to comprehend the enormity of what had happened.

The American people responded by rallying around their flag in a similar way to how the British public came together after the death of Diana. I believe the way that people reacted to both events can teach us a lot about human nature.

It tells us that in times of adversity we have a natural urge to connect with others and to share our experiences. Humans are very social beings and we find comfort together when we're in a flock.

The urge to bond and connect with others has been with us since the dawn of time. I believe that this is a natural urge that exists within us in order to help ensure our survival as a species. If you strip things down to the most basic level, it's obvious that no primitive man or woman could have survived on their own in the wild without the help and cooperation of others. It would have been impossible to hunt, build shelter, raise children and defend ourselves from predators if we were operating as lone individuals.

By coming together in groups, humankind dramatically increased its odds of survival. This is why early mankind formed into tribes in order to learn to hunt and gather food together. These bonds are extremely powerful and have existed throughout history.

We still see the tribal urge manifesting itself all around us today. It's apparent throughout so many walks of life. It's the reason why people experience so much shared passion at things like huge sporting events, religious gatherings and military parades.

If you've ever been part of a large crowd at a football game you'll know how easy it is to get caught up in the emotion of the event. I believe what happens here is that we feel a limbic connection with our fellow fans. You can hear the crowd gasp and cheer in unison, and grown men and women are capable of displaying great passion.

People feel great loyalty towards their team and their fellow fans, which is a modern manifestation of the tribal instinct. When our team does well, we feel good. When they play poorly, we feel down.

I read an interesting debate on a message board recently during which football fans tried to explain why it meant so much to them to support a particular team. When they analyzed it, most people agreed that they had very little in common with any of the players whom they cheered.

After all, it wasn't as if they knew any of them personally. Nor was there much affinity with the management of the club itself. In the end, most of the fans on the blog seemed to agree that what really mattered to them was an emotional sense of belonging to a common group with a shared sporting history.

It's not just at sporting events that this phenomenon is on display. When an audience sways in unison at a huge rock concert, there's something far more fundamental going on than people merely listening to music. The crowd is actually getting a huge buzz from the emotion of the occasion, and it operates on a limbic level.

In the UK, the 2012 Olympics had a similar unifying effect on the nation. The country came together to support the success of its athletes and the glow that the public experienced for several weeks as a result. Meanwhile, people form themselves into groups at almost every opportunity, whether they're built around work, hobbies or other interests. It's a natural urge to seek out the company of our fellow beings.

This goes some way towards explaining the reasons behind the modern explosion in social media platforms. If you think about it, the upsurge in things like Facebook and Twitter are no surprise at all because they promise to fulfill a very natural urge (although, as I've previously stated, Facebook can also be an instrument of disconnection).

Religion is perhaps the greatest example of people coming together to share a common set of beliefs and social bonds. As I said earlier, even though I'm not a religious person, I understand and recognize the benefit that many millions of people experience from it. I believe this is derived from the comfort they feel from the understanding that they're not alone in life. They have a higher power to guide them.

In my case, my higher power is the benefit that I experience from my limbic connection when I come together with fellow human beings in groups. When I walk into a meeting of a self-help group, I immediately feel at ease because I know that I'm not alone.

It's natural for human beings to seek out comfort through connections with others. It gives us a sense of belonging, and the cooperation that results has ensured our survival as a species.

This urge to interact also helps to explain why family bonds are so powerful. I think it's self-evident that the love and affection that can be generated by family links can have a huge positive effect on our mental wellbeing. Of course, the flipside of this is that both religion and family can be a massive source of distress if we come into conflict with the bonds that they create.

Ironically, religious ties have often resulted in wars and conflict – the very opposite of what the great theological belief systems set out to achieve. In my view, it doesn't matter which faith you follow, as long as you believe in a power greater than yourself.

Exploring Human Nature

What we're really talking about here is human nature. I believe that it's a human need to feel loved. I believe it's a human need to connect and interact with others. I believe it's a human need to feel valued and cherished as a person (both by our own selves and by others). By understanding these needs we can achieve true spirituality, which is a state of serenity.

> Everybody has a need for love and belonging. The opposites of these things that we depend on are loneliness and isolation, which are perhaps the enemies we fear the most on a visceral level.

Addiction is an illness that has solitude at its heart, even though we may not realize it. We become cut off from the real world and divorced from others. Some of the toughest-looking alcoholics that I've ever encountered have been reduced to tears in therapy sessions when they finally acknowledge this. In these situations, I simply ask for permission to hold their hand, which is a very tactile thing to do.

I then tell them: *'If you don't want to, you need never be alone again.'*

The effect that this piece of advice has on people can be very profound. We all want to feel that the people around us care about us and that we care about them. In other words, we're inter-dependent on others for our need for love and affection.

We therefore place a high regard on what other people think of us, even if we don't consciously acknowledge it. In the distant past, our survival as a species depended on these things, and as a result they've become ingrained within our limbic system. Indeed, our emotional welfare is *still* dependent on them. It's therefore only natural and logical that we should be on guard against anything that affects our emotional welfare.

The human condition is to be sensitive towards anything that threatens our basic needs as human beings, or which has the potential to harm our emotional health. This includes worrying about what other people think of us.

I believe this is a universal phenomenon that affects everybody, not just addicts. This means that to a degree we're all codependent on others for our needs. However, if you're born with an addictive nature then, as we discovered earlier – you become *super-sensitive* to anything that might harm your emotional wellbeing.

In other words, you develop full-blown codependency. In primeval times, being super-sensitive would have been a highly prized skill, hence the emergence of a section of the population that I refer to as 'The Watchers'.

The problem is that it cannot easily be turned off. Modern descendants of The Watchers are therefore left in a constant state of anxiety, which operates on a largely subconscious level through their limbic brain. If this is aggravated through childhood trauma, the feelings it creates can be unbearable, both in childhood and during later life. The result is that we seek to ease our distress by dulling down our pain through addictive behaviour.

The fact that the human condition is a universal state means that we all have the potential to be influenced by addictive traits, regardless of whether or not we're a Watcher. It explains why even non-addicts occasionally have one drink too many, or are susceptible to addictive urges. However, in these people the addictive behaviour does not become a life-dominating compulsion.

I believe that it's only through a greater understanding of the human condition that addicts can learn to rebuild their lives. Society must also accept that addiction is a widespread affliction that's grounded in human nature.

The way I think of it, it's normal human nature to be codependent with a small 'c'. This is because we all rely on others to help with our needs, and for a proportion of our self-esteem. We feel good when other people like us, but healthy individuals also have their own inherent sense of inner self-worth (which is where they differ from addicts, who suffer from low self-esteem). We must all learn to accept that we're all special by virtue of being human, regardless of our creed or culture.

Addicts are people who are Codependent with a capital 'c'. We're often totally reliant on others for our sense of self-worth – and if the affirmation we seek isn't forthcoming we can go off into a very dark place. This might mean that we must learn to live with unresolved issues, because life isn't always perfect. There will be ups and downs along the way, some of which we will find distressing, others exhilarating.

At the beginning of this book I stated that addiction is both a curse and a gift. It's a curse because it can ruin our lives and it allows our destructive demons to feed on us. But at the heart of addiction lies sensitivity. If we learn to accept and embrace this sensitivity then I'm convinced we can turn our addictive nature into a very special gift.

In order to do this we must do two very important things:

We need to learn how to love and respect other people. And we must learn how to love and respect ourselves.

References

1. Obesity figures, UK: www.bhfactive.org.uk/userfiles/Documents/obes-phys-acti-diet-eng-2013-rep.pdf

2. Cost of obesity, UK:

www.nice.org.uk/nicemedia/live/13974/61622/61622.pdf

www.bps.org.uk/sites/default/files/images/pat_rep95_obesity_web.pdf

3. Cost to UK NHS of alcohol abuse:

www.nhs.uk/news/2011/05May/Pages/nhs-stats-on-alcohol-hospital-visits.aspx

4. Obesity figures, USA: www.cdc.gov/obesity/data/adult.html

5. Child obesity figures, UK: www.bbc.co.uk/news/health-16175387

6. Facebook growth: www.bbc.co.uk/news/technology-19816709

www.insidefacebook.com/2008/08/19/mapping-facebooks-growth-over-time/

7. Household debt figures, UK: www.bbc.co.uk/news/business-25152556

8. Opiate/Crack users, UK: www.nta.nhs.uk/facts.aspx

9. Drugs deaths, UK: www.telegraph.co.uk/health/8595115/Britain-has-highest-number-of-drug-deaths-in-western-Europe.html

10. Alcohol deaths, UK: www.ons.gov.uk/ons/rel/subnational-health4/alcohol-related-deaths-in-the-united-kingdom/2011/alcohol-related-deaths-in-the-uk--2011.html

11. Smoking deaths, UK: ash.org.uk/files/documents/ASH_107.pdf

12. Obesity deaths in the UK: www.nhs.uk/news/2013/08August/Pages/new-US-estimates-link-obesity-to-18-per-cent-of-deaths.aspx

www.noo.org.uk/NOO_about_obesity/mortality

13. Illicit drug use, USA: www.samhsa.gov/data/nsduh/2k11results/nsduhresults2011.htm

14. Prescriptions issued in UK for the treatment of alcohol dependence: www.hscic.gov.uk/catalogue/PUB10932

Appendix 1

Suggested Reading

The Intimacy Factor: The Ground Rules for Overcoming the Obstacles to Truth, Respect, and Lasting Love, Pia Mellody (HarperCollins, 2003)

Facing Codependence: What It Is, Where It Comes from, How It Sabotages Our Lives, Pia Mellody (HarperCollins, 2003)

Facing Love Addiction Giving Yourself the Power to Change the Way You Love, Pia Mellody (HarperOne, 2003)

Breaking Free: A Recovery Workbook for Facing Codependence, Pia Mellody (HarperSanFrancisco, 1990)

You can find details at www.piamellody.com

Understanding the Twelve Steps: An Interpretation and Guide for Recovering People, Terence Gorski (Prentice Hall/Simon & Schuster, 1991)

Passages Through Recovery: An Action Plan for Preventing Relapse, Terence Gorski (Hazelden Information & Educational Services, 2008)

You can find details at www.tgorski.com

Why We Get Fat: And What To Do About It, Gary Taubes (Anchor Books, 2012)

Good Calories, Bad Calories: Fats, Carbs, and the Controversial Science of Diet and Health (published as *The Diet Delusion* in the UK), Gary Taubes (Anchor Books, 2008)

You can find details at www.garytaubes.com

Suggested Viewing

Sugar: The Bitter Truth, by Dr Robert Lustig: YouTube presentation available at http://tinyurl.com/ldgu9k

Appendix 2

Self-help Fellowships

The following self-help groups may be of interest to people suffering from addiction and / or their families (we addresses may vary depending on which country you are based in. If in doubt please google name of support group):

Alcoholics Anonymous – www.aa.org

Alcoholics Anonymous (UK) – www.alcoholics-anonymous.org.uk

Al-Anon Family Group (support for friends & family of problem drinkers) – www.al-anon.alateen.org

Al-Anon UK (support for family & friends of problem drinkers) – www.al-anonuk.org.uk

Anorexics and Bulimics Anonymous – www.aba12steps.org

Cocaine Anonymous – www.ca.org

Cocaine Anonymous UK – www.cauk.org.uk

Co-Dependents Anonymous (CoDA) – www.coda.org

Co-Dependents Anonymous (CoDA) UK – www.coda-uk.org

Debtor's Anonymous – www.debtorsanonymous.org

Debtor's Anonymous (UK) – www.debtorsanonymous.org.uk

Eating Disorders Anonymous – www.eatingdisordersanonymous.org

Families Anonymous (Global site for relatives and friends of people with drug or related issues) – www.familiesanonymous.org

Families Anonymous (UK site for family members of people with drug issues) – www.famanon.org.uk

Gambler's Anonymous – www.gamblersanonymous.org/ga

Gambler's Anonymous UK – www.gamblersanonymous.org.uk

Marijuana Anonymous – www.marijuana-anonymous.org

Marijuana Anonymous UK – www.marijuana-anonymous.co.uk

Narcotics Anonymous – www.na.org

Narcotics Anonymous UK – www.ukna.org

Overeater's Anonymous – www.oa.org

Overeater's Anonymous UK – www.oagb.org.uk

Sex Addicts Anonymous – www.saa-recovery.org

Sex Addicts Anonymous UK – www.saa-recovery.org.uk

Sex & Love Addicts Anonymous – www.slaafws.org

Sex & Love Addicts Anonymous UK – www.slaauk.org

Shopaholics Anonymous – www.shopaholicsanonymous.org

Appendix 3

Addiction Case Studies

The following case studies were written by recovering addicts. Their names have been changed in order to respect anonymity. Their experiences are by no means limited to drugs and alcohol, but include a whole range of processes.

Peter (mid thirties)

My name is Peter and I'm a Compulsive Overeater, Anorexic and Bulimic.

I was always an anxious kid. I don't remember a time when I didn't feel awkward or unsure of myself. I was the youngest child – and the only boy. I lived with mum: a loving but fiery woman who married and divorced my dad, an older intellectual.

He was a brilliant man – but crippled by self-doubt. He became both God and Monster to me, while I became my mother's hero, the 'miracle son'.

My sisters came with their own issues. When they weren't raging at each other, they raged at everyone else. It was a turbulent place to grow up in, but today it's hard to be angry about that. I didn't know it back then, but my parents both had their own difficult childhoods.

By the age of five, I knew I was different from other boys. I had a crush on Christopher Reeve's Superman, and would leave my bedroom window open at night for him to fly in and 'rescue' me, which seemed an entirely natural thing to do.

It wasn't until other boys noticed my difference and labelled it 'queer', and me as a 'gay lord', that the bullying began. On my first day at primary school, I was hit by a football, and I burst into tears. It was probably an accident, but I was so oversensitive, I presumed everyone hated me, which set me up for life.

Up until the age of seven, I was very creative and highly imaginative. I loved words and music and books and stories. I recorded tapes, interviewing friends and neighbours. I wrote and performed plays and poems. I saw the world through made-up words and funny voices.

Mum wanted me to be the 'man' of the family and daydreamed about me training as a doctor so I could buy a sports car to chauffeur her round town. It was not to be my fate, but I suspect this was one of the many reasons I grew up thinking I was a failure. It was around then that I started overeating at mealtimes and craving sweets and chocolate after school each day – which I was given money for. As mum worked late, I had to walk home on my own.

When I was ten, my headmaster came to my house to tell my parents he thought I was gay. Horrified, I listened from the stairs as he told them my biggest secret. My world came crashing down. I was called in and told I should not 'choose' to be gay as 'homosexuals were the most unhappy people in the world'.

He pronounced the word with such clinical hate – like a 1950s newsreader. HOMM-O-SEXUAL. I was terrified. Of course I denied it. Traumatized, I shook and cried hysterically, but no one told me I'd be okay.

By now, I was always eating. Sweets, chocolates, fries, pastries, sugar, junk food, fried chicken… whatever I could get my hands on. Eating numbed out my feelings. It made me feel better. I became the class clown to rebuff the bullying – now made worse by my weight. I put myself down before others did. I stole money from my mum's purse to buy sweets and friendships. I went from a small, gentle, sensitive, sweet, creative boy, to a loud, obese, attention-seeking troublemaker within a year.

At some point, I also went from 'comfort eater' to 'compulsive overeater.' Mum tried to get me on diets, but I failed miserably. Alcoholics and drug addicts steal for their habit, and I was no different. I stole food from my friends' plates and from the canteen. I raided friends' fridges at sleepovers. I 'borrowed' money from their parents for the 'bus fare' home. At meal times, I had seconds, thirds, fourths and fifths. The bigger I got, the more I hated myself. And the more I ate to cover the pain.

I was a small kid in height – I stopped growing when I reached 5ft 5 ins – but by the time I was 14, I'd hit 15 stone, and I don't know how I managed to carry the extra weight. Somehow, I scraped through my exams and went to college, where I was much happier and finally came out. I even lost some weight. But my addiction to food didn't go away and I went back to bingeing.

When I was 17 I made some friends, and we started going to gay bars. It was exciting, but I felt so out of place among the sea of toned male flesh. I'd found my people, but still I didn't fit in. While my mates were making out with guys on the dance floor I'd hide in the corner, planning my next binge. Soon, I added alcohol to the mad mix. It made my world more fun – or so I thought.

If sex happened – which was rare – it was in a dark corner with a drunken stranger for a quick fumble. In my mind, no one wanted a short, fat, hairy boy. I was no good at relationships, so I used self-deprecating humour and my own body weight to keep anyone from getting too close. The more I thought they rejected me, the more I ate. I hated my body, and so I ate more still to escape the pain. Utter insanity. I wanted to stop – but I didn't know how.

In my 20s, I found that I could lose weight momentarily. This was achieved by starving myself and restricting my calorie and fat intake – excessively. Years later, I learned that I was merely acting out my anorexia – the other end of the disordered eating spectrum. I didn't realize that any periods of 'controlled' eating were simply followed by longer periods of a 'loss of control.' I'd lose three or four stone in a matter of weeks, but then swing back to secret bingeing and put it all back on again.

For the next 15 years, my life was spent in an utterly insane and miserable cycle of overeating, anorexic dieting, compulsive exercising and binge drinking. When I wasn't eating, I was in on my own, getting drunk, or spending several hours a day in the gym. This dramatic yo-yo dieting distorted my body image, and damaged my body, inside and out. Yet that still wasn't enough to stop me from starting again.

In bars, guys looked straight though me – perhaps I represented their own fears about weight. I despised being fat. And yet, on my way home,

I'd buy a bag of binge food to make myself feel better. Later, I learned to vomit in order to make room for more food. By then, I'd developed the classic 'three-sided coin' of disordered eating: bingeing, starving and purging. I had all three symptoms and I never knew which side the coin would land on. I had no control at all.

I lost and gained weight at least 10 times over a decade – swinging from 18 stone back down to 11 stone within months. I'd binge, feel disgusted, starve and then do it all again. Friends wouldn't see me for weekends on end if I was 'in the food'. The shame I felt was intolerable. When I did surface, I was coming down from sugar or booze, so I'd argue and scream my way into yet another drama.

I reached rock bottom in 2007. My weight had peaked at over 19 stone. My stomach was so large, I hadn't seen my penis in years. I often wet myself before reaching a toilet, and I had difficulty wiping my own backside.

I ended up in a sex club, staggering around the floor in piss and vomit. I'd been drinking all night and passed out. I remember waking up in a sling, and then I blacked out again. Then I woke up in someone's bed. I've no idea what happened in between. The next day, I stopped drinking and I haven't drunk since.

An amazing doctor who was concerned about my weight mentioned the 12-Step group Overeaters Anonymous to me. Desperate, I began attending their meetings and 'working the steps'. I began to lose – and then maintain – my weight in a way I'd never achieved before. It was a miracle.

Over time, I found abstinence from eating behaviours and foods that had held me prisoner for years. Today, beyond the food, OA has helped me to address the thought processes which, as an addict, have robbed me of many years of my life. Food was once the solution to numb and sedate intense feelings. Now I recognize it as merely the symptom. The real problem lies in my thinking – which is slowly changing.

Years ago, I abandoned a very frightened but wonderful little boy. And now I'm getting him back. I'm sad that I left him alone for so long. He doesn't deserve to be put through the wringer in yet another binge-purge cycle. He deserves so much more.

Keith (early forties)

My name is Keith and I'm an addict. I will always be an addict.

I grew up in South Africa in the 1980s – a life in the sun, on the beach, carefree. I sailed through school and university with good marks, scholarships and bursaries. I got drunk a few times and smoked a bit of marijuana, as most teenagers and students do, but I certainly never had 'a problem' – at least not with substances.

Having an extremist nature, I never did things by halves. When I started modelling and partying during university, I discovered I really enjoyed it, so I stopped studying. I ruined four years of study because I'd found something I'd rather do – something that filled the void that studying didn't.

But, despite all the partying, I knew I'd never do ecstasy, cocaine or heroin. To me, they were hard drugs and I'd never put my prize asset at risk: my brain was my future.

On completion of my studies, I went to work for De Beers as a Particle Physicist, and a combination of awful management and a job that felt too much like hard work, led to me quickly becoming demotivated and susceptible to alternative means of escape. One night, while I was chatting to a rave DJ friend, he offered me half a pill of ecstasy and I took it… and my life changed!

Around this time, I picked up a girl while high in a nightclub, and two weeks later, her father and I set up a screen-printing business. Not being one for deliberation, I left De Beers to start working for my new company. But I'd never tried selling things before, and on the first day of my new 'job' I realized that I *hated* selling things, and quit.

And so began a few years of drifting. I modelled, played an extra in a soap opera, escorted girls in a beauty pageant, did stunts in a movie, became a rave DJ, bought a mobile disco business, became a chauffeur, worked for an event management business… among other things.

Unsurprisingly, it was at this time that I started using coke. It's also when I met Anna, who was working as a tequila girl. I was running a rave club and doing quite a lot of coke. I'm ashamed to admit that I persuaded Anna to do drugs with me, precipitating a downward spiral that made everything that came before look like carefully planned life choices.

Our relationship was screwed up at best, and exceedingly dysfunctional at worst. It was over within three months, but it took us eight years to actually end it. The reason we stayed together – the *only* reason – was the drugs. We went through the using phase, the abusing phase, and the addiction phase.

Needing to fund our habit, and as a result of my previous achievements as an honours student, I managed to land a job in investment banking. I became an investment banker from Monday to Friday and a rave DJ Friday to Sunday, as well as doing event management and graphic design every night.

For a while it seemed to be working. I was promoted, headhunted from bank to bank, and to outsiders we appeared to have it all: socially, financially and career-wise – a dream lifestyle.

In fact, it was no dream – it was a complete nightmare! Behind closed doors we often spent weeks living on soup and bread, having quite literally blown my not inconsiderable salary up our noses. Our relationship had deteriorated into bitter hostility, each of us blaming the other for the drugs, our problems, the hideous reality our lives had become... and the downward spiral continued.

There was another problem: the drug dealers' phone numbers were burned into my brain – there was no point deleting them from my phone. There was no escape from the misery of the life I was living.

I moved to London, where I couldn't just call the dealers, and I thought my addiction was finally behind me. Right from the start, I was going out every night, spending over £100 on alcohol and getting completely plastered. But at least I wasn't 'using', or so I thought. What I didn't realize was that my addiction, my desperate pursuit of escape, had merely taken a different form. I was as much of an addict as ever.

Within a few months, I was using coke again and my life slipped away from me once more. And then I met Kira. I was drunk and high that night – which elevated the encounter and seemingly intensified our connection. Almost immediately she started staying over at my place a lot, accelerating the development of our relationship.

Kira didn't do drugs; in fact she hated them. She moved into my place 'officially' after about two months, and in order to avoid arguments, I would do drugs behind her back. At night, as we watched TV together, every half an hour or so I'd go to the bathroom and do a line of cocaine off a CD cover I'd hidden there.

And so things progressed: the relationship, the drugs, the deception, and the guilt. I was getting drunk and high most nights, and every day I stumbled to work thinking: *Look at yourself – and look at the pathetic loser you've become, when you could have been and done anything with your life.*

At that time, I'd already started seeing Dave – a psychologist who specialized in addiction. His counsel was excellent, but all the advice in the world amounts to empty words if one isn't ready to hear them.

Friday, 29 February 2008 saw yet another big party at my place: more sex, drugs and rock 'n' roll. The next morning was business as usual – clean up the mess, lie to Kira, go and see Dave. There was nothing tangibly special or different about that day or that therapy session, but when I got back home and faced Kira, I became overwhelmed by guilt and remorse, nauseated by the lie I was living.

I broke down and confessed everything – the whole sordid truth: the drugs, the deception. She was furious, disgusted and disappointed, and stormed out of the house. But when she returned, she had a plan: *'We'll beat it together.'*

And so we began!

It was tough… and a blur. I can't even remember all of the things that happened, but I do know that Kira gave up her friends and her social life in order to help me. She stayed home on weekends and forced me to stay with her, and I cursed and swore at her – I wanted to go out and have fun with my 'friends'.

I started going to Narcotics Anonymous meetings the first Tuesday in March, as well as Alcoholics Anonymous on Saturdays. These became my regular meetings – I took strength from them because when I was at the meetings I wasn't using. There were good days and bad days; days when I had cravings; days when I wanted to use; days when I burned up inside.

But I didn't use. I'd get up every morning with one thought in mind: *Higher Power, help me stay clean today! Just today! Just until I go to sleep tonight! I can use tomorrow, but just for today, please help me stay clean.* And when I went to bed each night I'd read my Narcotics Anonymous 'Just for Today' reading and thank God that I hadn't used that day. I saw my sponsor regularly; I saw my psychologist regularly.

Days turned into weeks, weeks turned into months, and months turned into years. Kira and I got engaged. I hadn't known that life could be so good. I was finally living the life I'd coveted so many years before.

And then, with just over two years' clean time, my world fell apart! Kira left me for someone else!

My entire existence ground to a halt. I was shattered, destroyed, crushed! How could this happen? She was the reason I'd stopped drugs. We were perfect; we had beaten my demons together – what about our future?! My reaction was that of a shocked addict... my life was over, there was nothing left for me. If I were ever going to use again, it would be now.

But something inside me had changed. Granted, Kira was the foundation of me getting and staying clean to that point, but those years of being clean, of working the programme, of therapy, and of addressing the causes of my addiction had done their work. I was able to feel the pain but not give in to the compulsion to use drugs to numb that feeling.

Dave once said to me: 'You're an addict. You'll always be an addict. Your first thought and your first reaction to a stressor will always be that of an addict, but you don't have to act on that first thought. Think again and act on the second thought, not the first.'

And that's how I choose to live this life, this second chance that I've been given. Some days are good, and some days are bad. Life happens. I have a job I love and a great boss.

I have a fiancée – Kathryn – someone I've known for years and love madly; someone who is my best friend, sex goddess and soulmate all rolled into one. I have a family who support me unconditionally; they too know my demons and love me more for the fact that every day I choose to overcome them.

Ironically, I also own a flavoured vodka company; I've never tasted my products and hopefully I never will. I'm often told that, by putting myself so close to alcohol, I'm gambling with my sobriety and my future, and they may be right... only time will tell.

For now, I'm living in the moment. I've accepted who I am, and I'm grateful for all of my experiences – both good and bad – for they're what has shaped me into who I am today. I'm thankful for everything that I am, and accepting of everything that I'm not.

I have the ability to think. I have the ability to act: the ability to *react*. Most of all, I have the freedom of choice. I can choose whether the addiction will run my life, or if I will. Today I choose me; tomorrow I get to choose again.

This is dedicated to my amazing mother who died shortly after this article was written. She finally knew the truth before she passed on.

Gemma (mid twenties)

I'll start at the beginning of my life, because I believe my addictive behaviour started before I picked up drugs. I was born in Milan, Italy, in 1987, to an English mother and an Italian father. One of my most significant early memories is of being taken away from my dad (who was an alcoholic) and my home to live in the UK with my mum.

My struggles started in early childhood, as my mother became extremely depressed. My parents' relationship battle continued, and I was the weapon. When I was eight, I was moved to London to join my mum, after having been in the care of friends and neighbours. I was bullied at school. I was a good girl; I never dreamed that one day I'd become an addict.

With hindsight, the ill treatment and neglect I suffered at the hands of my parents was so severe that it was no surprise that I began to develop an inherent sense of shame. Bullies at school pointed out what I'd already learned to believe about myself: that I was 'unlovable', 'unlikable', 'different', 'a freak', 'ugly', 'fat', 'stupid'.

As a child, I couldn't intellectualize what was going on and tell myself that this was about them and not about me. The world was becoming an intolerable place. I took each comment that was made to me and swallowed it down with the rest, hoping that day would be the one that I was left alone.

I started developing an illness that my mum called 'a nervous tummy ache', and which I now know to be fear at the pit of my stomach. I'd pretend to be sick so I could stay at home alone. This became my sanctuary. My mum went to work every day and I spent hours watching films – they would take me away from the world. As my mind switched off, so did all those horrible feelings.

In 2001, I went to live with my dad in Italy. As a teenager I adapted to each situation in ways that would shield me from having to suffer on a daily basis. Starting a new school became the perfect opportunity to re-create myself. The establishment was old-fashioned, and smoking hadn't yet been banned from school premises. There were drugs all over the school – to the knowledge of most of the teachers. There were no rules, and no one who would hold me back.

I began smoking cigarettes and marijuana straight away. They not only helped boost my social status, but also switched off my mind. I wasn't vulnerable anymore; instead, I treated others how I had been treated. I didn't care and I blamed my parents. I became a good liar and a good manipulator. I felt older than my years, despite being just a child.

I picked up my first drink at a friend's birthday party. I'd already smoked pot that night, and I threw up everywhere. But still I kept drinking. I'd never even acknowledged the fact that I was gay. Older men knew how to take advantage of me. To me, it was an easy exchange to get what I needed: attention, drink and drugs.

I drank and smoked pot daily, and I was always seeking out the next drug. At 15, I convinced a fellow pupil to bring cocaine into school. I snorted a line in maths class. On my 16th birthday, during a night out with my friends, I exchanged my body for ecstasy. I had absolutely no idea what these drugs did to me, and I didn't care.

At 17, I moved back to the UK and reverted straight back to my old habits. I started seeing women. My first girlfriend was completely out of control, much like myself. By the time I was 18, I was consuming large and dangerous amounts of ecstasy, cocaine, amphetamine. And I tried crack for the first time.

I wanted help and I looked for it, but no doctor would provide me with a diagnosis. I was frustrated, because I knew it was abnormal to suffer the way I did. There was clearly something wrong with me and no one could see it.

The consequences of my using got worse, as did my inner turmoil. I hated myself. I self-harmed with kitchen knives – slicing through my arms to the point where I needed stitches. On my 18th birthday, I ended up in an ambulance after a three-day binge.

Another night, I thought it would be fun to climb on top of a friend's van while he was driving and jump off. When I landed, blood poured out of my skull. My so-called friend wouldn't take me to hospital, and so I lay in bed, vomiting and unable to move for days. Months later I got a CT scan and it revealed that my skull had been severely fractured; the impact of the fall 'should have killed me', according to my doctor.

My mum had kicked me out by this time. I had no home, and I was a park bench drunk at just 18 years old.

In the summer of 2007 I kept a diary with me because I was convinced I'd be dead before my 21st birthday. I'd given up. My mum was desperately trying to help me, but all I could say to her over the phone was, 'I'm beyond hope, mum.' When I finally agreed to let her pick me up, she and my granddad took me to a top psychiatrist, who diagnosed me as an 'addict'. I believed that my problems ran deeper than my misconception of what addiction is, so he elaborated: 'If you want another definition, how about feeling avoidant?'

On 24 September 2007, I went to rehab for the first time. I was introduced to a group of fellow addicts: bulimics, anorexics, heroin addicts and alcoholics. I was introduced to AA meetings. Rehab wasn't what I was expecting: an instant fix or wonder pill that would solve all my problems. Instead, I was faced with the one thing I'd run away from my entire life: my vulnerable self, much like the 11-year-old girl that I hated.

I discovered that I had problems with alcohol, drugs, relationships, sex, food, shopping, caffeine and smoking. The only addiction I didn't have was something I'd never tried: gambling.

I didn't stay clean immediately. After five months of recovery, I thought I could have a glass of wine. After a three-day binge of drugs and alcohol I ended up in hospital. I went back into treatment, this time in South Africa. I realized that the party was over – that relapse almost cost me my life.

My 27-year-old sponsor and mentor was one of the young people who inspired me to pursue recovery; I wanted what she had, and did everything she did to get it. I spent my 21st birthday in rehab, and slowly started to believe that I could have a life. With nothing to lose, I pursued that dream. I became passionate about recovery and I discovered my voice. I sought to help as many young addicts as possible. A feeling of esteem started to grow from within, and already I felt like a different person.

Recovery has been a slow and painful process. I've made so many mistakes, yet however painful those mistakes were, they moulded me into who I am and who I am yet to be. It's taken years to be free from the chains of my past. Today I'm six years' clean. I've finally found love, and a career working in schools telling my story and teaching drug facts to children.

I can do anything and go anywhere. I'm in control of my life, something I could never comprehend when I started this journey. Through desperation I walked the path of recovery blindly, often being held up by my peers until I could see the path in front of me. I don't have to stay away from a drink, because I don't want it, and for someone like me that's a true miracle.

Carlos (early thirties)

Growing up with a history of active addiction on both sides of my family, and in a town with one of the biggest breweries in South America nearby, it came as no surprise that I started hitting the bottle very early in life.

Drinking alcohol to the point of oblivion was, and is still, perceived as a sign of masculinity in Colombia. So, at the age of 13, impressionable teenage boy that I was, I had my first 'proper' alcoholic drink at a festival. Most of my friends and some family members were there, and I proceeded to black out and vomit in front of everybody.

To my surprise, my behaviour was not frowned upon. I also enjoyed the feeling of temporary numbness it gave me, as well as the sense of being rebellious and more of a man. Needless to say, I saw that incident as a green light, and drinking to the extreme became a sort of routine. I also remember that I thought that if I only drank on Fridays and Saturdays, it would all be well – another sign (I know now) of problem drinking. If you don't have a problem with alcohol, why would you start making rules about drinking it?

To my surprise, Fridays and Saturdays quickly became Mondays, and sometimes Tuesdays, and the new rule was that as long as I could get away with it and no one noticed I was tipsy or smelled of alcohol, everything was good. I would also like to say that at this point my drinking was almost exclusively social – another reason to think that it wasn't a problem – and getting together with people who drank to my level also supported that belief. It was fun, and the consequences were not then 'too serious'.

Without my noticing it, my academic success (I'd always been an excellent student) started declining. I was not the first clarinet in the orchestra where I played anymore, and I made myself believe that it was due to favouritism, and not the fact that, at 15, I had shown up tipsy to a few rehearsals.

My motivation and enthusiasm for my studies, which I actually loved, didn't seem to be there anymore, and a thirst for parties, and for social acceptance in the 'cool crowd', seemed unquenchable.

At the end of High School, and still not knowing what I wanted to study at university, I decided I was going to be a doctor. This seemed the acceptable thing to do, and also what would please my parents, especially my father. It was at university that I discovered marijuana, and how cheap and widely available it was.

I could now drink most weekends and smoke marijuana occasionally during the week. Surprisingly, I did pretty well for the year I was there, but I was too confused, and after a heart to heart with my mother I decided I wanted to be a veterinary surgeon. So, off I went to vets' school, only to repeat the pattern a few years later.

I think it's important for me to make the connection around compulsively 'quitting' plans and goals and drinking and using drugs. I believe my lack of determination and focus was greatly due to my substance consumption. It seems so obvious to me now, but back then it would have been impossible to even *try* to make sense of that link.

Drinking was a great tool for socializing, and for feeling part of things, and growing up as a gay man in a homophobic society, the need to belong and to feel accepted was sometimes too much to bear. I do think alcohol saved me from isolation and depression, and it was also a great ally while it worked.

After dropping out of university for a second time, I was sent to England: to broaden my horizons, to learn a new language and to live in a different culture. Little did I know that the British drank as much as the Colombians, and that alcohol and drug consumption was not only accepted, but encouraged.

The club scene welcomed me with open arms and I was then introduced to ecstasy and cocaine. I never used drugs more than my peers did (although I certainly drank more than all of them), so the illusion that I was not 'as bad' as the rest was still there.

The consequences of my drinking, however, started to become obvious. Blacking out was part of going out, as was losing my documents and mobile phone, and sometimes even ending the night in hospitals covered in bruises, or at police stations reporting a crime. I was never violent, but I did put myself in very risky situations where, inevitably, I would end up a victim.

My health also suffered. While I was drinking I would get a cold at least once a month; if I got a little stressed my skin would break up in eczema, and the athlete's foot I caught at a swimming pool in my late teens never cleared. As a by-product of drinking alcohol I also smoked tobacco, so chasing after a bus for a few feet always felt like running a marathon and deep breathing was a luxury I could hardly ever afford. And I was still only in my twenties.

Mentally, I was generally unhappy, too. I worked in a retail job I hated, and was surrounded by people who hated their jobs too – let's say that customer service was not our priority. I completely lost sight of any substantial goals in my life. I forgot I enjoyed studying, playing music and making art. I was seriously emotionally anorexic. I never had a romantic relationship that went further than a second date, and I made myself believe that casual sex was all that I was worth.

My last night before getting sober was not an unusual or a dramatic one. I went out, drank more than I promised myself I would, blacked out, lost my phone, fell on my face somewhere and woke up with that same old sense of dread – of knowing that if I didn't stop I would hate myself more and more, and more.

I found sobriety through a 12-Step programme nearly six years ago, and the meetings have been vital to my recovery. I remember the sense of defeat I had when I first attended one. I felt my life was over, that I could never be socially active again and that it would just be boring. However, it wouldn't be as boring as waking up wanting to die, so I stayed.

To my surprise, things only got better and better. I'm now as healthy as I can be. My skin has completely cleared; I get a cold every one or two years; and I don't smoke or do drugs. I'm also at college doing a foundation year in Art and planning to do a BA in Fine Art. I'm surrounded by loving and understanding peers who understand me at a level no one else could before. I'm also in a new romantic relationship that's loving, and in which I'm learning tolerance, respect and boundaries. I'm happy and optimistic, most of the time.

It hasn't been an easy ride – if anything it's been challenging – but with all the tools, love and support I've been offered it's a real fact of my life that today I can be happy if I choose to. At the moment I'm doing my steps in the money fellowship, and it astounds me that all that love and wisdom that I found in the alcohol fellowship is also widely available for all types of addiction, be it under earning, gambling, other drugs, sex and food disorders, anything!

Doing the steps, taking service commitments at meetings and being in contact with my sponsor are at the core of my recovery. Being honest about my feelings and where I am at in life have allowed me to establish real connections and to get, and offer, help. Asking for that help and accepting my vulnerability have also been a real lesson for me.

I had my first therapy session nearly a year into sobriety, when things felt a bit flat, and it has made a real difference ever since. Being in therapy has helped me understand how I function, how I make mistakes, how trauma works, how codependence is at the core of addiction, and also that there's a solution. It has basically taught me how to love and how to feel compassion for others and for myself, and to accept how imperfectly perfect we all are.

The motivation and focus that alcohol and drugs took from me are slowly but surely coming back into my life. By staying sober I'm making ongoing amends for the harm that I caused to my family and friends, to society, and to myself on a daily basis.

By staying sober and in contact with a power greater than myself (call it 'other people trying to lead a healthy lifestyle', God, the universe), I'm useful to others and find a real sense of joy and purpose. And by waking up sober to whatever challenges I might face every day, a day at a time, I feel that my life is definitely worth living.

Paula (late thirties)

Everyone says that I was born an addict. I've spent years trying to figure out how my life ended up here, but I realize now that it's not important. What matters is *this* is what I am. If I look back, I really did seem to have it all. An amazing family, a loving older brother and incredible parents. Looking from the outside in, it seemed pretty perfect. In reality, I was going through a horrific trauma, but I decided the best way to deal with it was to keep my mouth shut.

I grew up in Hong Kong and my memories of my childhood are of sunny days spent on the beach, surrounded by friends. I experienced sexual abuse between the ages of five and nine. Even at that age I was full of shame. I became quite clever at hiding my emotions, and my dress sense changed – I thought if I looked like a boy and made myself unattractive the abuse would never happen again.

It was from that point that I went on to self-destruct. It started with an eating disorder and then developed into self-harm. I struggled to talk to teachers or friends about it – I was too ashamed to admit the truth of my situation. I'm a very sensitive person – as I guess most addicts are – and the fact that I couldn't cry or show emotions came out in rescuing stray, beaten-up animals. I spent every moment I could, trying to bring them back to life. I realize now that I was doing for them what I couldn't do for myself.

School was hard. I'm not academic and I just scraped along. I was drinking at this point – as were the other kids. The safety of Hong Kong gave us the freedom to go out most nights without our parents worrying. By the age of 13 or 14, I was hanging out on the beach, drinking and smoking cigarettes and spliffs.

Everyone was doing it, and I didn't want to be left out. I would turn up to school just to be with my friends, as well as to skive off to meet with my boyfriend, who had been kicked out for dealing and taking drugs.

My brother developed an illness around this time, so my parents' focus was very much on him as they travelled around the world trying to find the right treatment. I was left to my own devices. I wasn't a bad child and I was constantly trying to please everyone around me. The problem with that was that I lost myself in the process.

Later on, I threw myself into drama, which really helped as I could pretend that I was someone else for a while and it allowed all my emotions to come out. If I had another chance now I would have continued down that path. Unfortunately, drugs came along at the same time. I had the opportunity to go to university, and for the first time I had made my parents really proud. By this time I was 17, and although life seemed great from the outside the reality was that I was already falling deeper and deeper into the depths of addiction.

Things later took an awful turn when my best friend's father died of a heart attack in front of us. We were both in shock and I guess emotionally we froze. She asked me to get hold of some crystal meth. A friend of mine gave me a couple of bags, assuring me they were meth. They weren't, they were pure grade heroin. Unfortunately, the minute we tried it, we lost the choice to put it down, it was that powerful.

Over the next couple of years things got progressively worse. My parents found out about the drugs and I was kicked out. I lost the opportunity to go to university, as I'd decided that it was far more important to become a heroin addict than anything else.

The girl who was my best friend overdosed one night on the side of the street and my priority, instead of saving her, was to strip her down to get her drugs before the police or an ambulance turned up. Nothing was more important than my next high.

My friend didn't make it past 24 years old, but even that wasn't enough to stop me. Each time I tried to get honest with my family and check myself in somewhere for help, the drugs were more powerful than my intentions, and I would end up running back to a life I hated. I was given so much love and so many opportunities, but they weren't enough to beat the feeling that I got from the drugs.

I always ended up using again, and I put myself in dangerous situations in order to get drugs. Eventually, I fell pregnant after a horrific incident in the UK in which I was gang-raped by three men while I was on drugs (I still regret that this was my only chance to have kids).

After that, I tried to get my life together and I succeeded for a while. I had 10 years clean, between the ages of 24 and 34. My life really took off – people believed in me, which in turn helped me believe in myself. I became a fashion designer, living all around the world and experiencing amazing countries and amazing people. I taught myself everything I needed to know so that I could be the best I could at my job.

For a while, things went really well. I forgot all about my addiction, and that was the problem. Once the drugs were out of my system, I was left with me and my emotions, and I didn't know how to handle them.

At the age of 34, I started using drugs again. I'm 39 now, and still battling this horrific disease. What I realize now is that, since I was a child, I've been running away from me – from how I felt and from what I experienced. It has taken me 15 treatment centres and being surrounded by caring and professional people to understand this.

Before my last major relapse, I was living in California and was surrounded by opportunities and amazing people who wanted to help. But my loneliness took over and I hooked up with some guys I'd met in detox. My experience over the next six months is hard to put into words.

I came from a loving family; I grew up with the world at my feet, and I never thought for a moment that I'd end up like the junkies I saw begging and stealing on the street. Using my body to get me that five-minute fix and hating myself for it. I ended up in jail on drugs charges. I was petrified, dope sick, and surrounded by strangers. I had no shame. This is what drugs had done to me.

After coming out of jail I didn't think I could get much lower, but I underestimated the power of my disease. I lied my way into a few hospitals, with no money and no identification. I just needed my fix; what people thought about me didn't matter anymore. I ended up letting men use me, and I even risked sharing needles, knowing people were riddled with hepatitis C and God knows what else.

I didn't think I had that much longer to live, and to be honest I didn't care, if that was what my life was going to be like.

Eventually, I returned to the UK, where my family was now living. It was then that I hit a complete emotional rock bottom and I considered throwing myself under a bus. Thankfully, my family intervened, and they gave me another chance by sending me into a treatment centre. I have been in recovery ever since (subject to a few bumps along the way).

My life is not what I ever imagined it would be, but I'm alive today with an incredible story to tell – to help others and be there like people were there for me. Recovery has given me amazing friends who love me till I can truly love myself. It has given me an inner strength that's indescribable. It has given me a willingness to fight, but more importantly it's given me hope.

I shouldn't be here. I've ended up in comas, I've overdosed and I've been in car crashes. I've done things to my body that I'm not proud of. I've lost many of my friends through this disease, but I haven't lost myself. Each day, by sharing my story, it teaches me acceptance and gratitude. I have an amazing book of life and for that reason I am truly grateful.

ABOUT THE AUTHOR

David Smallwood has a Masters degree in Addiction Counselling and Psychology, a post-graduate diploma in Therapeutic Counselling and a diploma in Counselling for Addictive Disorders. He has trained in EMDR (Eye Movement Desensitising and Reprocessing) and PIT (Post Induction Therapy) with Pia Mellody at the Meadows treatment centre in Arizona. He has worked as a treatment director in two rehabilitation clinics, and as manager of the addiction unit at the Priory Hospital North London. David is currently the Treatment Director at One40 Ltd, Harley Street, London, and specializes in addiction issues and treating any childhood trauma that has led to anxiety and depression.

 www.one40.org.uk

 one40recoverycommunity

 @One40RC

www.davidsmallwoodtherapy.co.uk